TEMPUS
Oral History
SERIES

TROWBRIDGE
voices

Two characters from *The Flag Lieutenant* production by the Trowbridge Amateur Dramatic Society at the Town Hall. Charlie Taylor is on the right.

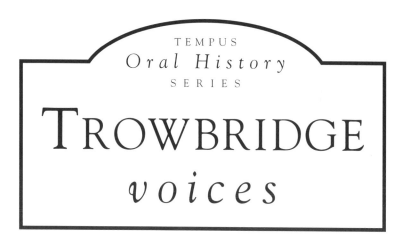

TEMPUS
Oral History
SERIES

TROWBRIDGE
voices

Compiled by
Ruth Marshall

TEMPUS

First published 1999
Copyright © Ruth Marshall, 1999

Tempus Publishing Limited
The Mill, Brimscombe Port,
Stroud, Gloucestershire, GL5 2QG

ISBN 0 7524 1644 8

Typesetting and origination by
Tempus Publishing Limited
Printed in Great Britain by
Midway Clark Printing, Wiltshire

I would like to dedicate this book to my mother, Betty Doig, who sadly is not here to see or read it, but who was responsible for nurturing in me a deep love of history.

CONTENTS

Portrait of the May family. Bert May, the baby, later became a well known local figure, working on the *Wiltshire Times* staff and as an active local preacher and Sunday school secretary at Wesley Road Methodist church.

INTRODUCTION

As a child I often sat with my brothers and sisters in the flickering light of a coal fire, as my mother told tales of life in 'the olden days'. She recalled days before cars and television and a life far removed from our own experience of childhood in the late '50s and '60s. She talked of days during the General Strike, when her grandfather, a station master, dared to work and how she was stoned and spat upon once when out walking with him. She told us about life in a convent school and the attempts to turn 'little Betty' into a young lady – attempts that, she said, always failed miserably! We were intrigued by her exploits during the Second World War testing tanks with the Inspectorate of Fighting Vehicles. All her papers showed her as being over five feet tall and yet she never in fact reached four feet eleven and often required a box to stand upon!

She was a great story teller and had the knack of making us feel as though we were there, experiencing it all – the sights, the sounds and even the smells, of a lifestyle long gone. Many years later I came to realise that this was 'oral history'. The sort of details that the history books don't tell us can be supplied from memory by those who actually lived through the changing ways of life and we should take the opportunity to listen and record them when we can.

Having spent more than ten years nursing elderly people, I have heard many fascinating stories and pored over boxes of photographs, putting faces to the characters described. My work in 'reminiscence activities' has developed this interest and it was a short step from simply hearing the stories to wanting to make a record of them.

The interviews for this book were collected over a period of six months and were conducted mainly in the interviewees' own living rooms or in the nursing homes where they now live. In transcribing the tapes of the interviews, I have made as few changes as possible to the words actually spoken – only just sufficient to make for ease of reading and understanding. The written word therefore is very close to the spoken one.

I feel privileged to have shared these glimpses into the past lives of some of the older residents of Trowbridge – I have often been amazed to hear how detailed memories can still be, even after seventy or eighty years. My eyes have been opened to a Trowbridge that I scarcely knew existed yet the remnants of much of it are still there if you care to look. I hope that something of this important past will be carried in these pages and that this book will not only remind some people of the way life was, but also help a younger generation to know what life and work in this thriving market town was like in the years before they were born.

I apologise if I have made any mistakes in the interpretation of the interviews or in the descriptions to the photographs – I have tried hard to check all the details wherever possible.

I would like to thank the *Wiltshire Times* for permission to use photographs covered by their copyright, Andrew Jones for access to the Zion church archives and Michael

Marshman and the Wiltshire Records Office for their support and the loan of recording equipment. Finally, I would like to thank everyone who has given their time and their interest, shared their personal memories with me and been willing to share them with a wider audience through the pages of this book. I also thank all who have lent me their cherished photographs and shared with me the delights of their family albums and scrapbooks. It has been a pleasure to meet the many contributors, most unknown to me before I started on this book, and I look forward to keeping contact with many of them in the future.

Trowbridge South East Football Club team of 1909/10.

CHAPTER 1

Childhood

Bill and Dorothy Avons photographed in Dymott Square, Hilperton, *c.* 1934.

Alice Porter riding her tricycle in Middle Lane, c. 1922.

Street Games

We played marbles and rounders and touch, hide and seek, that sort of thing. We always played football in the street. Sometimes we did play in Adcroft Street, most times we did play across the top of British Row from the Black Swan up to top of Charlotte Street. We had a high wall from the pub garden, it saved the ball going over that side and then we had railings on the other side.

Gordon Mundy

Playing Slacks

We used to play a lot in the streets. We used to play what you called slacks on the way to school. You'd throw your marble and the friend walking behind would try to hit it. If he hit it, he had another go. If you miss, then of course you carry on, and that's how we went to school, like that, going along the edge of the street. We got alleys from the brewery. They were clay made, you could buy those about six or seven for a penny.

Fred Hardiman

Flower Show Field

Living down Newtown was handy because we didn't have far to go to what we called the Flower Show Field, opposite the Trinity Church. We used to go down there and do handstands and they had swings down there. We used to play tennis, 'cept we didn't call it that- we called it bat and ball. We used to spend hours down there.

Lilly Pickett

Tops and Hoops

There was a factory at the bottom of our street, what they called the rubber factory. That's where we used to go out and play ball, out in the street and spinning the top and hoops- they were wooden ones. I had a doll and a teddy, I've always loved teddies.

Alice Smart

Court Fields and the Park

We played whip and top and hoops – both the wooden hoops and the metal hoops. The metal hoops had a fixed arm on it and it would run round as you did push it. We used to get the bottles, with the marble stoppers. In Court Street there used to be a mineral water factory and they used to use those bottles a lot. We used to go round there and we were always well supplied with marbles from them. The coloured ones were few and far between and they were expensive. We used to play in the park, no ball games were allowed in the park, only in the lower end which we called Court Fields. We used to play cricket and football in there, and where the Civic Hall is now, leading down long ways, that was the junior football pitch. They had junior goal posts there and they had big goal posts over the other side by the factory, Palmer Mackay's factory. Really until you were a big lad, you couldn't play over there – well you wasn't welcome, unless their ball happened to be sitting on the spikes of the railings and then they used to come over and you know what it is, you'd get a big lad against a small lad, we used to get pushed out the way or kicked out the way. The boating lake was there and we used to use it as a boating lake. Bits of wood with a piece stuck on upright, you know, improvised sailing boats, course they used to get stuck in the middle, so we used to have to get in after it. You used to have to take a chance whether you cut your feet or not, because there used to be a lot of glass bottles thrown in there. We had vandals in those days!

Jack Carter

Singing for Pennies

When I was about four or five my father used to play the melodeon at the George and I used to go over and sing. I remember Sharp's used to do an oval toffee tin and I remember having it piled high with pennies. There was always ways and means of earning the odd penny or two, running errands across town or whatever.

John Reynolds

The Time of our Lives

I was born in Dursley Road and from there the whole family moved to the Ring O' Bells in Hilperton Marsh. We had a marvellous time at the public house, because there was a large garden and lots of extra rooms where we could play hide and seek. We did hopscotch and skipping and leapfrog. I joined in all the boys' games. I used to do handstands up against a wall. When we were back in Trowbridge, everyone seemed to congregate in Waterworks Road after tea, and we had the time of our lives. Playing marbles or skipping. I had a friend who had the most marvellous scooter and I clung to her, because it was such a lovely thing, we never had anything like that. We used to have races around the block, one would go one way and one the other.

Enid Hill

Games at the Cloth Mill

We used to go down to the mill when we were small. We were

Children play outside 18 West Ashton Road. Mrs Lillian Taylor is visible in the doorway.

very naughty. They had their own hose pipes there, their own stirrup pump in case of fire. The hoses were made of a canvas or hessian then. On a weekend we used to get these out and drag them along the floor. They were awfully heavy to hold when the water came through. Being a small child, I can remember it almost jumped out of my hand with the force of the water through it. Sometimes the water got onto bales of wool and we got told off for that. Another trick we had was to go into the wool shed. The huge great bales of wool used to come there before they were processed through the mill. It was full of rats. We used to go and hide in there and chase each other round and there were these rats all over. I wasn't a bit frightened of them.

Anne Mackay

Tea from the Pail

My mother used to do washing and all sorts of jobs. She'd take in washing from the barracks for the soldiers, the Royal Horse Artillery. I used to have to collect the bundles of tablecloths from the barracks in Frome Road and mother used to wash them. Then they had to go back and when I took them, I used to go in the mess and I'd get a cup and dip into the pail of tea. They made their tea in a stainless steel pail. They used to look after me a little bit. I would have been between twelve and fourteen.

Jack Carter

Paper Rounds

I was doing a paper round from eleven years old. You know the corner of Bythesea Road and Mortimer Street, well there was a paper shop there – Mr Trollopes the name was. We had to be down there at six o' clock in the morning. He'd already have gone along the railway station and got the papers. They were generally in by half past five, he'd bring them back and sort them out into the order of the houses, so we could do them without looking, more or less. He always had them sorted for us. I used to start along Bythesea Road, I had four or five houses along there, go up Stallard Street, down Bradford Road, Innox Road, then come up Westbourne Gardens, West Street. Into Gloucester Road, down Westbourne Road, up Avenue Road to the top, then you'd go through the cut to Pitman Avenue. Go up Pitman Avenue, round down Frome Road, along Bradley Road and my last ones were Holbrooke Cottage and a bungalow about ten yards from Silver Street Lane. I can remember every step of it now! I had a bicycle, it was about fifty six papers, and I got 3/6 for that for the week. Then you'd get a paper bag and go round the shop picking a handful of sweets here and there and that was your bonus. The family always enjoyed them.

Later we had our own round – *Wiltshire Times* on a Friday, whether my older brothers did start it for pocket money I don't know. You could go up the *Wiltshire Times*, see, and buy so many papers. You'd have to pay a cheaper rate and then you'd go round delivering them. A small round, but that got you a bit more pocket money for after school. It was always published Fridays then.

At Charlotte Street I'd get home about eight o clock from my paper round and if mother wanted something

Jessie Whitmarsh enjoying a run out with her parents in the Morris Bullnose.

for dinner, we always had to go down to Cleveland's the butchers, for stewing steak or something. That was in Silver Street. So we went and got it and took it back. If mother looked at it and it weren't to her satisfaction, we had to go back with it. I expect they were open about half seven, but I always worried about being late for school.

Gordon Mundy

Knocked Down by a Tin Lizzie

As a very small boy, there was not much traffic and in 1917, I got run over. What a hue and cry that was – from what I gather: I was killed and everything! We lived in Upper Broad Street and the school we went to was

Lilian Almond walking in Middle Lane with Alan, Raymond and Marian, 1946.

the top of Timbrell Street, the new building. Course we used to go up there you see. The cars in those days, they were Fords or called Tin Lizzies. Apparently I was running along to school, one afternoon and I was knocked down by this Tin Lizzie, quite close to the school. I was taken to the Rose and Crown pub in Timbrell Street. I was knocked unconscious. At that time the hospital was on the corner of the Halve and I was taken from the pub into the hospital. When I woke up, there was I in a cot and Mum and Dad were both peering over the top. I was in there for about four or five days, then I came home.

Fred Hardiman

Toy Trains

I think we had a nurse or something to look after us in those days. She came by the day. People did have nannies in then. We were probably with her more than we were with our own parents, you know. At the far end of Courtfield House there were three rooms that we could play in, that was our nursery when we were very small. It was quite cut off really. We would go up there. My brother was very keen on engines and he had a railway track and one of those engines that you fill up with methylated spirits. The blooming thing sometimes used to fall off the track and get on fire. The floor up there was something akin to lino, so it didn't actually burn. We had toy fairs, on little wagons and they used to go from room to room, and we'd say that they were going from town to town. Our parents would let us do that. They were very good with us, like that. We used to assemble all these fairs. They had little roundabouts and things. They must have been bought. There were many things like that in the shops. I think my brother had made the little trailers out of Meccano and we'd go from room to room and have the fair in the evening. We'd have some music of some sort – an old wind-up gramophone probably.

Anne Mackay

Money for the Pictures

We used to collect jam jars and rabbit skins to get our money for to go to the pictures. We used to take them down to Pike's on Back Street, a rag and bone yard there. We'd go round the neighbours or anywhere, that was what we had to do if we wanted money for the pictures. Saturday afternoons for the silent films. We had Tom Mix and a few more of them, with a little man playing the piano. We always used to call him Jesus, for some reason or another.

Jack Carter

The Isolation Hospital

We had a box, a sort of cardboard box with a slot in the top – it was the hospital box, we used to call it. I suppose it paid for our doctors bills, but we weren't interested at that age. At one time there was scarlet fever, an epidemic of scarlet fever about, and I was prone to tonsillitis every Spring,

Mrs Lillian Taylor enjoys a walk with a young Bob Taylor in the pram.

about March. This year I was taken to the Isolation Hospital, St John's now. I can remember being in there in a side ward all on my own for a week or more, while they took tests, but mine wasn't the scarlet fever. There was a chap, Arnie Woolley, he was just a few years older than me and he was always whistling and he was in the hospital. He'd had this scarlet fever and he was getting better, I could hear him whistling out there in the ward.

Gordon Mundy

Chores on the Farm

From about twelve I always used to cycle to school. There was no traffic, no traffic at all on that top road.

Children could walk and cycle anywhere in those days. It was about five miles into school. My mother had a lot of poultry, so before I went in the morning, I used to have to help with the poultry. Take some food up to the hens and let them out. In the holidays I used to do that three times a day, let them out in the morning, collect the eggs in the afternoon and shut them up and fasten the houses up at night. My brothers started helping with the milking when they were about eleven or twelve. Farmers' children did have to help on the farms then, this is going back to the thirties.

Vera Taylor

Anne and Donald Mackay in Dutch costume for the Trowbridge Carnival children's fancy dress, early 1920s.

Cigarette Cards

I was always interested in wildlife, flowers and that, and one day I found some orchids in the field behind the school. That really excited me. I knew every wild flower there was, because we used to collect the cigarette cards. There was a wildflower series, and I used to study them.

Max Connor

Last out of the Park

We used to go down the park and play games with a bat and ball and hide and seek. The park was all railed in, right up to the last war and then they took the railings away. There were gates and before the war, we had a park keeper and at a certain time in the evening, he used to blow his whistle and you all had to get out. Then he locked it up. We used to see who could be last out when the whistle went. Half way down to the lake there was a wall with railings all along there and you could go down in the bottom half any time and that was just a field.

Jessie Whitmarsh

Country Jossers

We used to go for long walks. From Hilperton, we went up Steeple Ashton Road, come back along the West Ashton Road and back through Trowbridge. Sometimes we were allowed to pick the primroses in the woods at West Ashton and we used to bring them back for the old people that couldn't get out. Also on that walk, there was a field filled with beautiful cowslips and 'Goosey Ganders', wild orchids in other words. We used to go across there and pick up basketfulls. Or if we went picking violets or primroses, they all came back, blackberries and things like that – proper old country jossers way.

Dorothy Walton

Playing in the Lanes

The games we used to play usually were outside. Our garden was only small but we seemed to have nearly everybody in from the whole neighbourhood when we played at our place. Most of our friends lived 'up the lane', as we called it. Bond Street has several little lanes that go through to Waterworks Road. There's Lower Bond Street, Upper Bond Street, Bond Street Buildings and we would play in the lane in between. Sometimes we might be privileged to play in somebody's yard way but usually it was in the actual lane itself which were really only little dirt tracks.

Lynda Bosworth

Magic Lantern Shows

My brother did magic lantern shows from about the age of twelve. There was a long room that was originally part of the weaving sheds, but no longer used. He built the whole thing in there himself and had a projector – 9.5 film I think, quite a narrow film in those days. He would hire old Laurel and Hardy films, things like that from a shop in Bath. He used to show these films and local children would come in and pay tuppence. He had some music and I used to get behind the curtains and just when the film was starting, I'd have to pull the cord to open them. I used to take a tray of sweets round, you know a penny a bar or tuppence a bar. I can remember that. All the old films he used to show. Sometimes the film would come off the reel and end up on the floor – that was a mess! These films were only hired and had to go back in good condition. At the end of the film they all had to be rewound. He did that for quite a few years.

Anne Mackay

First Car Ride

My first ride in a car, it was an old Ford T you know, a bakers van it was. He used to come around with a horse and cart and then suddenly he turned up with this van. Mr Rose of Shails Lane it was. 'Twas only a matter of getting in the car and going from the Three Horseshoes up to Bythesea Road – about fifty or sixty yards, but nonetheless it was my first ride in a car. Tin Lizzie's that's what they were, they used to come from Germany and they were made out of proper tin.

Jack Carter

Margaret and Arthur Jones, c. 1919. Margaret later married Sidney Hardiman and was mother to Lynda and Ruth.

Collecting Numbers

We lived in Heywood and from an early age I used to go up on the Navvy bridge and collect train numbers. Most of the kids were into that before the war. I remember before I went to school, our dad gave me a pedal car for Christmas, made of metal and I used to pedal that up to Navvy Bridge and run down the other side. There was no fear of any traffic. There were only two people in the village had cars at that time, that was Mr Betteridge and Mr Jenkins. I used to go down to the little river bridge, Horse Bridge, and I'd go down there with a notebook and take car numbers. That was on the Yarnbrook to Westbury road. Many a night I'd sit down there for two to three hours and go home disappointed, because I hadn't seen a single car! I'd very often walk up to the railway station to get the engine numbers and I had two or three experiences that kids would be glad of today. I rode on two footplates. One was a Castle class locomotive and one was a smaller one. I'd ask the drivers if they'd give me a ride and sometimes they did.

Max Connor

Penny Overweights

I always remember very vividly, there used to be someone in the market hall making sweets, boiled sweets. They had bits like skeins of wool, and they used to throw them over a hook to mix the colours up. Then eventually he'd have it all strung out and then he'd cut them up with scissors and you'd have your boiled sweets. We used to go in there during the lunch time or break time from school and used to always have a couple of sweets. Other sweets – we had what we used to call locusts, which was like a brown stalk actually. It was a ground root and it had like some seeds inside, imagine a dried up french bean, well it was very similar to that, but not so big. It was sweet, really sweet. We used to get those in overweight packets. You'd go in the shop and have a penny overweight or a ha'penny overweight. That was – they used to do up packets a ha'penny or a penny, and they used to put all odd sweets in a paper cone. You never knew what you were going to get in there and you had either a ha'penny one or a penny one, all according to what you could afford. It was overweight because it was more value than what you would have got for a straight bag. They used to put all the leftover bits in, I imagine, but none the less it was good value.

Jack Carter

We saw the Queen

Major Mackay lived at Hilperton House. The family owned what was Court Mills. He was a generous benefactor, he used to have the children from Hilperton School in his dance hall for a Christmas party. You'd come back with an apple and orange and nuts and stuff. I can remember Queen Mary coming and we were all lined up there, down the road, the Knap. She was a very tall lady, very stately and upright – she looked around. I think it was just a favour by the Major for the school children.

Dorothy Walton

Short of Toys

I was born in Whaddon. There were five children all under seven and my mother had quite a time with us actually. My father was a farmer. I don't know what we did play, because we didn't have any toys in those days. In the 30s, even the farmers didn't have much money. My mother didn't have any money to spend on us, so we were

very short of toys or books or anything. From about ten I used to have library books, my mother always had library books, she always read a lot. The library was on the bottom of Wicker Hill, where the road bends round to the right.

Vera Taylor

We all had Chores

I had to help to clean the cutlery and help wash up, normally. We had to take our share of the household chores, it wasn't a case of having a meal and going out to play. Even lunchtimes before you went back to school, you had to wash up the dinner things.

Jack Carter

Dirt Roads

The roads weren't made up, they were dirt roads, dirt and stone. In the Summer they had the watering cart out to keep the dust down. We'd run under it, try and get ourselves wet. Eventually they had macadam roads. I think it was put from the Town Hall to Trinity Church, so that was marvellous. They'd say, 'Have you seen that new road?' and gradually they came all round here. Before that, you could get ever so muddy and the people wore gaiters and the girls wore things with buttons up. They were ever so hard to do up, but you didn't get so muddy. It was quite a different way of life.

Grace Marsden

A children's Christmas party held at the Lamb public house towards the end of the Second World War.

Film Shows and Christmas Parties

Around about Christmas time, the youngsters of the town used to get invited into the Market Hall, to sit down at these trestle tables and have our tea. So far as I know it was the Chamber of Commerce used to provide it, the business people used to take it in turns towards this. We used to sit in there and have a nice tea and come away with a bag of sweets, an apple and an orange. A couple of times we went across the road to the Picture Palace, the Palace Theatre it was then. We used to see lantern shows at the Salvation Army hall. Used to pay a penny to go in there on a Monday or a Tuesday evening and they had the old projector way up in the gallery at the back and the screen down there. What they used to show I haven't got a clue! Anyway we used to go there. They also used to have lantern shows in the hall which was adjoining Fear Hills shop – Hills Hall, I think it was called.

Jack Carter

Visits from Grandmother

My father's mother and father lived in Holt, they had moved from the farm and had a house at the top of the hill, a very old house. My mothers' parents lived at Steeple Ashton and my grandmother used to drive a pony and trap, and would drive from Steeple Ashton to Whaddon to come and see us. Children were quite in awe of their grandparents in those days. We didn't go very often to see them. My father used to take us occasionally to see his parents. We always went there on Christmas Day, in the evening. All the children and grandchildren would go. We used to have a stocking on our beds, but there wasn't a lot in it. It was filled up with an apple and an orange and dates and things and then we would have one toy, and as there were five of us, we didn't get much in the way of toys. We didn't miss it because everybody was the same.

Vera Taylor

A Broken Arm

I can remember breaking my arm and waking up the village with the screams. I was going to fetch some oil for the lamps from the shop at the top of the village. On the way back there was this motobike coming and I ran backwards and forwards and I slipped on the gravel and broke my arm. My father said that he could hear me right down at the public house. So I got whipped off to Dr Wright, who was the doctor in Wingfield Road and he examined me and I had to go straight to the hospital which was then in the Halve. I was operated on as soon as the doctor had finished surgery. We got taken back in a horse and trap, which my father had.

Enid Hill

Fishing in the Biss

We'd go fishing in the Biss. We used to go into the hedge and break a stick off and get some cotton and a bent pin, dig for some worms and go after sticklebacks. There used to be quite a lot of sticklebacks and newts, all that sort of thing down there. There used to be a little stream going off, behind the boating pond and that's where we used to go fishing. Put them in a jam jar.

Jack Carter

Ushers' Bottle Tops

An interesting game that the boys used to play – they'd go round to the bottling plant at Ushers and beg or steal coloured caps that they put on the beer bottles, the sort that you've got to get off with a bottle opener, and they'd play almost like a game of marbles with them in the drains. Roll them along. They used to come to school, not with pocketfuls of marbles, but with pockets full with these bottle tops.

Marion Dutch

Fire!

We came into Trowbridge for the Flower Show and my father came

Enid Bathard standing in Bunce's Farm field in 1931. It later became the Frome Road football ground.

to pick us up after we had watched the firework display. It was rather late when we got back, I remember looking for the chamber pot and I had a quilted bedspread and one of the tassels happened to go in the bowl of the little lamp and the next thing I knew it was on fire. You were sleeping on straw mattresses in those days and the straw began to go up like mad. I remember having a real good hiding that night, for being a naughty girl. I can well understand it, because my hair was loose and I was in a flowing nightie. There was only a very tiny space between the wall and the bed and my father and aunt were very annoyed because they burnt their hands trying to put the fire out.

Enid Hill

A Spike Through my Leg

One day I do remember in particular was a day when I was eight years old – I wasn't particularly ladylike in those days! Just up from where I lived in Bond Street, there were some garages with stakes in the ground where they would hook over the garage doors when they drove the cars in and out. Every time I came up the road, I would divert off the footpath and across to where these were and I would jump from one spike to the next spike. I'd done this so many times but on this day, the Sunday school anniversary day, I jumped and I missed the last one and the spike went into my leg. To this day I still have the scar. It's about two and a half inches long. I can remember screaming and dashing down to my dad and he took

one look at it, took his big handkerchief out of his pocket and tied it very tightly and said, 'Right, quick, in the car'. He was one of the few people who had a car – because he was a rep'. We dashed down to Trowbridge Hospital and there was Dr Napthe. She quickly sized up the situation and got out her great big needle and went in and out and in and out with two great big stitches and big knots at each end and then a great big bandage around this leg. She said, 'There you are, you'll be OK'. This was all in the lunchtime. When I got home and I said, 'Oh Dad will I be able to sing this afternoon now I've got that on my leg?' He said, 'That won't affect your voice of course you can sing' and I did, including a solo. You always sang a solo if you had a loud voice and I was one of those.

Lynda Bosworth

CHAPTER *2*

Schooldays

Children at the Parochial School in 1923. Jack Carter is second from the left in the middle row.

Children of Miss Say's class at Parochial return from a PE lesson in the gymnasium at the Tabernacle church, 1959.

Pot-Bellied Stoves

Hilperton school was up by the church. The head master was Mr Pearson. They were all older teachers. I started when I was three and you had to have a lie down every afternoon. Miss Chapman was the teacher then. Then we moved up to Mrs Pearson and then Miss Berett come. That room had a partition; there was three classrooms. We had blackboards and the old fashioned pot-bellied stoves. The toilets were bucket toilets and then you had to wash your hands in cold water, where you hung your coats. We played hopscotch, whipping tops, skipping ropes. We had to stay in the playground but the boys were allowed out on the Knap, so they played all sorts of games. For school you wore anything, there was no such thing as school uniforms. You wore black shoes, black stockings or navy blue. Sorts of thing that didn't show too much dirt, I think it was.

Dorothy Walton

Caned at Three Years Old

We went to school in Park Street. We had a Miss Weller as our teacher. They were disciplinarians. We were only little but we had to take our outside clothes off and hang them up. We had a special place and if you didn't do it properly you were caned, even at that age. You could go to school at three, but I was just over that, about four. I remember once, I could have been about five and a half, when we had long metal desks, my foot slipped off the metal and made a noise in the class and she came and hit my foot.

I went on to Parochial school eventually. I quite enjoyed school and did all right at school really. The girls were that side and the boys were that, and never the twain should meet. Anyone who was found climbing up to look into the girls playground, ooh, it was a terrible offence. It was awful to think they had climbed up to look to see what the girls were doing. It was very rigid and very prudish, I suppose you might say. We were brought up very much to be circumspect, and that.

Grace Marsden

St Thomas's School

I went on to the Parochial school, but first I went round to St Thomas's to begin with, at three years old. It was a little place through the Armoury. Just by the bottom of the Halve there was a cut through, St Thomas's Passage, and there was an oldish building, a sweet factory, and next to it was the little Parochial school, a one storey building. We went there and then went to Parochial proper at five or six. There was a Mrs Jones, taught us. It was a very small school, just one or two classes.

Gordon Mundy

We Had Inkwells

We all played, boys and girls together, at Margaret Stancomb's. I started when I was three or four. It was a nursery school in them days and I was there till I was seven. I learnt to write on one of those little slates and we done most of the things they learn today. We didn't have to keep changing our classrooms, the teachers come to us. We had desks to keep everything in. They were all in one, the desks, in a line, and we had inkwells. You went on to write with a dip pen, they tried to encourage you to. Of course you got more blobs and mess on your page! We had the cane and if you done anything wrong you had to stand outside the headmistress's door and wait – and then you got the cane.

Mavis Burt

Spring Cottage School

I went to a little school in Ashton Street. It was two sisters – Miss Minty and Miss Violet, that was what we called them. It was called Spring Cottage School in Clarks Place, which was just off Ashton Street. They had quite a big house and the school was in a building in the garden. There was only about fourteen of us, a very small place, and we were from five to fourteen. I was happy there. We read the Bible every day and were taught on that and were taught geography, history, reading and writing – copperplate. The sisters had beautiful writing, but mine was never as good as it should have been. Yes, I enjoyed it

Miss Minty and Miss Violet Minty who ran the Spring Cottage School in Clark's Place.

very much and left when I was fourteen.

Jessie Whitmarsh

Taught to Behave Ourselves

I went to Parochial School from the age of three and I cried my eyes out when my mother left. There was a Mrs Berret who lived in Frog Lane and a Miss Perritt, she carried on teaching I think at Newtown Junior School afterwards. We had long forms with the long desks, rather primitive really. Just what we were taught – goodness knows, though we were taught how to behave

ourselves. Then I went on to school at Park Street, I went up there I think when I was about eight years old. The girls used to play this game throwing a ball up against the wall. We used to play marbles going to school in the gutter, as we went along and of course go into school with dirty fingers and get a couple of strokes of the cane. We also played football going to school, passing the ball from side to side – there was no traffic about then.

Jack Carter

Preparatory School

I went to a little school in Hilperton at the rectory to start with, when I was about four and a half. My sister was five and I went to keep her company. When she was six she was ill with a TB gland and so we both stayed at home for a year and we had someone to come and stay who taught us for that year. Then when I was about six, I started coming into Trowbridge with my sister. There was a preparatory school attached to the grammar school, the Girls High school. I was there until I was eleven and took the Eleven Plus and went onto the Girls High School. The preparatory school was in a hut on stilts. It was a very old thing, left over from the 1918 war, I think. It was a long thin building and had quite a few classrooms. It was mixed boys and girls, but then after eleven they divided up. When I was there I used to catch the bus to Hilperton, back from school, and then walk the last two miles. They had just finished the new building when my year was due to go up. The boys' school was the lower part and the girls part was the new building on the left. We had quite nice playing fields in those days with tennis courts; we had quite a lot of sport and gymnastics. We wore white blouses and navy gymslips, the blouses were square necked. They decided that it was more healthy not to be muffled up. We had cookery and sewing classes, we did a lot of subjects in those days. I loved my school days, because it was very isolated at Whaddon.

Vera Taylor

Cooking at Adcroft

We used to do cookery lessons, but we had to march from Newtown school right up to Adcroft. They had a room up there where they did take different schools for learning cookery. Miss Gore was their cook, but she was a teacher. If you could take things like flour or fat you could, but if you didn't have it, you could buy it from her for tuppence. We used to make a lot of cakes and then she taught us the way to cook potatoes and how to cook a

Charlie and Lillian Taylor with Denis on an afternoon out from Dauntsey's school, *c.* 1930.

Adcroft Senior Boys school football team who won the Wiltshire Shield in the final against Devizes Southbroom in 1936. Left to right, back row: Mr Bingham (headmaster), Barnes, Burden, Vince, Purkins, May, Knight, Mr Hibberd (sports master). Front row: Mundy, Charnbury, Wenham, Aland and Cookson.

meal. It was very interesting.

Lilly Pickett

No More Spit

Parochial was a lovely school. Mr Richards was the head who left and Mr Richardson was going to be the new one. We had a peripatetic head at the time called Miss Farley. Reggie Geer had come from London – he'd come down with a class of evacuees and then he'd stayed on at the school. There was Miss Smith, always referred to as little Miss Smith, she took 1A, Miss Jackson took the second year children, Mrs Fallowes, she taught the remedial – special needs you call them now, and Mrs Hole – now she was a character. There was one famous story told about her. Now, one boy was spitting at

somebody else, I think it was his favourite pastime, but Mrs Hole stood him in the corner with a jam jar and she said, 'If you're so fond of spitting, now fill this jam jar!' Eventually he turned round to her and said, 'I haven't got anymore spit!' and she said, 'Well, that will teach you a lesson.' She was full of stories like this. She really was a larger than life character. Although a lot of the staff were older, coming to the end of their careers, and a lot of us were young, we all mixed very well. They were very friendly and very helpful.

Marion Dutch

Afternoon Off

At the Parochial, we used to go across to St James's for morning service on Ash Wednesdays, football boots wrapped round our necks so that we could go down the Flower Show Field and play football. You had the rest of the day free, it was a special half day.

Jack Carter

We Never Mixed

We were segregated into two complete lots. The boys playground was the left hand side, the girls was the right hand side, we never mixed apart from during lessons. The classrooms were an old fashioned version of open plan, because the school is built like a cross and the cross piece was one huge room with two classes in the one room. We were just separated by screens. There was Miss Jackson and Mrs Cox, they were the two teachers. The headmaster was a Mr Bryant and there was Mr Geer, who came from London with the evacuees.

Stanley Jones

Gardening at Night School

At eleven you went on to Adcroft Boys. I can remember the teachers – there was 'Dotty' Taylor, then there

The boys' playground at Parochial School in 1963.

was 'Fussy' Watts, he was the English teacher. I always remember him, if you done anything wrong he slapped your hand with a ruler instead of the cane. Then there was 'Skipper' Angel, he was the strictest and he was always the most respected. You respected teachers them days, you didn't answer back. I remember 'Skipper' Angel, he'd walk round – if you were doing anything wrong, he had a ring on his finger and you'd feel that on the back of your head. The headmaster was Mr Bingham. The sports teacher was a man named Hibberd. We had English, arithmetic, gardening .

We played football on the school ground. For our school matches we used to go into what was called the King's Fields. The cricket club has taken it over now. Mrs King, she lived in a big house at the top of Charlotte Street, I think she owned the fields and it was always known as the King's Field. We took our cricket lessons over there.

Gordon Mundy

An Extra Bath

Adcroft School had a wash house across the way and every Friday they used to light up the boiler and there were two showers. Some of the people who liked to be clean, from the Conigre, would take their best towel, which was always a tatty old thing, to school on that day and we could have a bath there. We used to go to school very often on roller skates, but I suppose more often you would go to school kicking a tennis ball, backwards and forwards. You passed the girls' school on the way and chased a few girls and they'd run away and giggle and laugh.

John Reynolds

A class at Parochial school in 1947. The class includes some of the children evacuated from London. Alan Almond is in the front row, far right.

Getting a Good Report

We got reports. My report was always quite reasonable, except I always got written on the end, 'Wish she didn't laugh so much'. I always got that and my father used to say, 'If you don't get a worse report than that, I don't mind'.

Jessie Whitmarsh

Sports in the Flower Show Field

When I was five year old, I had to go to a little school down the side of Trinity church. When we had the other school built, up Newtown, we went to that one. After that, we had to go to the Newtown big school, the junior school on the main road. The teachers we had were Miss Bailey and Miss Wright. We used to have races on sports day, and we had to march and go down to the Flower Show Field for that, because we only had a playground and it wasn't big enough. The boys used to play football there as well. We did junior netball in the school, but hockey we used to go down the field, see.

Lilly Pickett

Play Times

There wasn't a lot of room to play anything very much in the playground at Parochial. The girls would occasionally play skipping and ball games and ally-ally-o and circle games and things like that. The girls playground was made even smaller, because there was a great pile of coke in the corner. I think it was originally in the boys playground, but the boys spent all their time climbing all over it, so it had to be transferred to the girls playground, because the girls played better and didn't want to get themselves dirty.

Marion Dutch

Evacuees at School

All my children went to the Parochial school, at the bottom of Church Sreet. They made this school over for the evacuees and I used to go down and meet the children out of school and you'd get talking to the other mothers, all evacuees. My daughter only stayed until the Juniors and then she went to Newtown and then to the seniors at Nelson Haden. Fifteen, the school leaving age was then.

Lilian Almond

Uniforms

At the Girl's High School, I can always remember the uniform was a white blouse and a navy blue gymslip and a green girdle or sash. The seniors could wear a tie, green and gold ties, and you had a blazer with a gold emblem on it. Velour hats with a band round and panamas in the Summer. The summer dresses changed twice while I was there. One was a plain green with a collar and I think the other was a green and white stripe with black stockings and shoes. We wore tunics with a slit up

Children of class 2A of Newtown Junior School 1952/3. Miss Norman is the teacher and Lynda Hardiman stands beside her in the middle row.

the side for gym. We had quite a bit of homework. They were strict, but they had a way of teaching you and there was respect on both sides. Miss Field was headmistress when I started, but Miss Dawes came afterwards.

Mary Martin

Thank God That's Over With

Every year when we broke up in the Summer, we gave the two Miss Mintys' a present. We had a collection and bought them silver things and a bunch of crysanth's usually. They got dressed up in their best clothes for that – it was very old fashioned, you know. We didn't have a uniform, but we had to wear hats and gloves and if we were on holiday and we met them, I used to say, 'Oh, no I haven't got my gloves on!'

We had panama hats in the summer and velour in the winter. We had badges with SBS in gold on the front of our hats. We had a little cloakroom where you could leave your gloves and hats. It wasn't a very big place and Miss Violet taught the little ones at one end and Miss Minty took the older ones at the other end. I dreaded going up to the older ones and then when I got there, she was nicer than Miss Violet. We had desks joined together in a line, with lift up lids and inkwells and forms to sit on. We stood round a table for lessons and they let you read round the table, taking it in turns. We learnt the piano – I didn't want to learn, but I learnt from five to fourteen and never touched it after that. I said, 'I won't play it when I leave' and I never did. We had a piano at home and I had to practice. At the end of the term when we gave them their present, one of us had to play the

National Anthem. It was my turn one day and my Dad said, 'Thank God that's over with!' – he'd heard me playing it so much at home.

Jessie Whitmarsh

The Bucket Brigade

You used to discourage them from going to the toilet as much as possible. The toilets were outside and they always froze in the winter. The funny thing was – the toilet paper was not kept out in the toilet. The toilet paper was kept in a cupboard, so the children would come and ask, 'Can I go to the toilet?', or, 'Can I go to the toilet with paper?' You had to issue out a few sheets of toilet paper to them. It was just taken as a matter of course, I don't think anybody was particularly embarrassed by it. If the weather was very bad and the toilets wouldn't flush because they were frozen, they organised the bucket brigade. The taps inside weren't frozen and they would fill up the buckets inside and go out and flush the toilet with these buckets of water. So at play times and dinner times you'd have this bucket brigade going.

Marion Dutch

Our King is Dead

I remember 1952. King George VI died and we were all presented with a small halfpenny stamp, with his head on and we had to write what we remembered about

him, what his life consisted of and what a good king he was and how the young Princess Elizabeth would soon be Queen Elizabeth II. I remember writing, 'This is a very sad day because our king is dead.' I think it was probably written on a blackboard and we copied it down and afterwards we had to write down any of our thoughts about it. This stamp, I've still got it, and the piece of paper that we wrote on. It was a very special day, although it was a very sad day. Mrs Rodway made sure that we fully understood the significance of what it meant.

Lynda Bosworth

The School Day

You had to do a dinner duty as well, which was awful. You had to stand

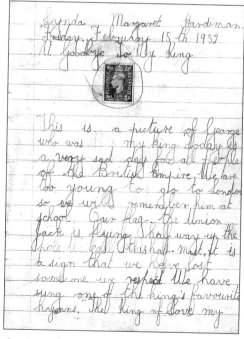

A piece of writing about the King's death by Lynda Hardiman, 1952.

Miss Ivy Hart with her class from Parochial during a visit to Lackham School of Agricultural in 1962.

there and make the children behave themselves and have them quiet to say grace before they started their meal. Doing your dinner register was a bit of a nightmare to get it to balance. The eldest child in a family paid so much, the next child – a penny less, and the next a penny less again. So all the children were paying different amounts of money.

Marion Dutch

I walked to School

At eleven I went up to Nelson Haden and I was one of the first to go when it was just built. I remember when I first went I had something wrong with my feet. I'd had an operation on them and had plaster on both of them. To get transport you had to be three miles from school and they came and measured it from St Thomas' Passage to Nelson Haden and we were just inside that three miles so I had to

walk. Nearly every week they had to take me to the clinic to have the plaster redone, because I'd worn the feet out.

Mavis Burt

Further Education

I started at what is now Trowbridge College – called the Further Education College then. I went there and the year I started was the year that they actually opened the college. Up until that time they had just rented rooms in Trowbridge all over different places. They had rooms at what was Adcroft School, which was like the boys section – all sort of building trades and those sort of things they did there. The Victoria Institute would have housed the clerical side of things and it was that I was going into. I did a two year course that covered secretarial, clerical – all the commercial sort of subjects.

Lynda Bosworth

CHAPTER 3
Working life

An early picture of workers at the Wyke Road brick factory.

Four Jobs in Two Years

My first job was at the Co-op, as drapery department errand boy. Cleaning windows, washing the step at the front and taking out four or five boxes of hats at eight or half past eight at night, because some of the women would come in right at the last minute and want twelve hats sent out on approval to the other side of the town and they must have them that night. It used to annoy me intensely. I had hat boxes on the bike so high, I'd have to lean round to see past the damned things. Then I would have to go and collect them all on Monday morning. From the Co-op I went to Yates's, who were bedding manufacturers, down at the bottom of Castle Street, opposite McCalls factory. I was working in the place where they punched holes into the metal for making the frames for the beds. Then they brought in a new welding machine – a spot welder. I was only fifteen and you weren't supposed to work on any machine until you were over sixteen. Anyway the engineer, Applegate, he lived along the Innox, he said, 'You're an intelligent lad, I'll put you on there.' There was a trolley in front of this machine, that you could put a bedstead on, the frame with the spiral springs, and the job was to weld the ends of the supports for the spirals. You just twisted them into these supports. I had a lad called Chris and he was in a skylarking mood, and I was clouting him when the boss came along and told me to take myself off, he didn't want me. From there I went to Church's – the butcher in Silver Street. I didn't stay there very long. My mates were telling me about the money they were getting at Nestle's, I was only getting ten bob, so one Saturday morning, with a basket full of meat to deliver, I rode across to Nestle's and tried to get a job. They kept me waiting outside until twelve o'clock and they rang up my boss and when I got back, they gave me the sack.

From there I went to Sainsbury's as an errand boy. Sainsbury's was down on the Town Bridge. They had a mill there and two shops, a grocery store and next to that they had the corn shop, that sold pet food and corn, dog biscuits, all that sort of thing. Bob Sainsbury began to take an interest in me and he used to come out and show me how to weigh up sugar and rice and things like that. He would stand and talk to me for an hour. There was another chap there who was very kind to me, Harry Wilson. He was on the meat and butter counter. He gave me a brown coat. Mr Reynolds was the warehouse man up top. To get stores from the bottom to the top, they had a lift and I used to go up and help him with the lift whenever he was pulling up stores from down below.

John Reynolds

Clocking on at the Mill

When I left school I went to work at Salters, which is now part of the Shires. When you went into a weaving shed you had to start at the bottom doing 'bobbing', which was weaving on the bobbin putting odd pieces of wool on, then you worked yourself up to 'tie-ers on' and 'drawing', then 'quill winding' and then you went to weaving. It was very interesting. It could be dangerous with the shuttles if they flew out, because they were capped with steel at each end. It was the old clock system, you had your clock card and number. I spent many happy years down there. In fact when you got married from there, which I did, you could go up and choose a piece of cloth. I remember I chose a piece of grey flannel and had a costume made by my uncle who was a tailor and a little hat to match.

Joyce Hunt

Working Your Way Up

I didn't know what I was going to do really, not for a job. My Mother said my sister and me, we had to go in service when we left school. My Dad's sister she went in service and she finished up as a lady's maid. It was a good job and my Mother said, 'If she can do it, you can do it.' Any rate, we didn't go in service, we both went in the factory. My sister she went in Clarks but I went in up Salters. I started at what they call 'bit winding', after that I went 'quill winding' – that was the quill that went backwards and forwards. You had so many weavers to look after, see. You had to put the quill into the right basket. The girls on the weaving gave us tips because the more quills you gave them, the more they could keep weaving without stopping. Otherwise if you haven't got enough quills for them they've got to stop, and they wouldn't earn their money then. I used to keep their baskets full and they'd say, 'Don't do any more, I shall finish my cloth with these.' I used to do very well on

Alice Chapman as a trainee nurse in 1925. She later worked at the Isolation Hospital in Trowbridge.

that and when Christmas time came I used to have ever so many tips, because I used to keep them going.

After a time they might say they need some 'tie-ers on', so we had to come off and we said, 'Yes, we'd like to do it'. Then we got stuck doing the serving and the drawing. And then after that, if they were getting short of weavers, they asked if we want to go weaving. Well, I used to do a little bit of weaving, when there wasn't much 'tie-ing on' to do. I used to go down with a friend and she used to show me the way to do the weaving. So when they asked me to go weaving, I more or less knew what to do

Jack Carter pictured beside the lake in Trowbridge Park in 1935. Note the mills of Palmer and Mackay with the chimney, behind him.

and they did put you on a slow loom then, to learn. Then they say you'm getting on alright you can go on a fast loom. It was alright. You get better work on a fast loom and you got better pay then. When I started down there I was getting 7/6. My sister, she started down Clarks, she was going to learn the way to spin, that's on the big mules and she was getting 5/- a week. You could earn good money on weaving see. You get a good 'quilley winder', keep you going in quills, you can do a cloth in two days. That's at least seventy yards. If you finished your cloth in the morning you got your money in the afternoon, so you could get paid a couple of times a week and then your bonus on top of that. It

might be 10/- or might be 15/- you'd get that Wednesday dinner time and that come in handy, see, in the middle of the week. We used to do some lovely exports for America – beautiful cloth for America. If you know you've got export, you know you've got a good bit of cloth. We used to do a lot of this small check, very nice that was. It's a pity that all these factories is gone, when you see what skills are wasted.

Lilly Pickett

Putting My Coat on Early

Dad was a loom tuner at Clarks, and then he went to Salters. That was making up all the designs for the cloth and keeping the looms in good order. Mum was a weaver and then she worked at Nestles. I worked in all the cloth mills in Trowbridge bar Salters. There was Kemp and Hewitts, Clarks, McCalls, Mackays and Salters. I first went into McCalls, but the money was so poor – I was 'quilley winding' and then I went onto weaving – four looms. Then I went on to Kemp and Hewitts and that was where I nearly lost this arm. I was in the loomshop where there was only one loom and I wanted to get away that night, early. My loom was still going when I put my coat on, but my sleeve caught in the belt, and they were massive big belts, and my arm went in. Luckily the coat wrapped all around the arm and I was just very badly bruised. But I never put my coat on early again. Of course they are automatics now and they shut off at the least little thing, but not then, they kept going until someone shut them off. It really was hard work and you earnt every penny you got. You got paid for what pieces you got made. I used to come home with about three pounds – and my mum had two and I had one.

Mavis Burt

A Bookie's Runner

At one time my father worked on the tarring of the roads, with a horse and cart. They had a tank on the back with a fire under it. It had a pump on it, to pump up the pressure to spray the tar on the road. This was in the Summer and I would have to take a cooked dinner to him every day in a basin with a bottle of tea. Whichever part of the town he was in, I would have to race over and find him. He was also a bookie's runner, he liked to have a bet. When I came home from school, when I was about ten, I used to have to run from the Conigre across town to Park Street or Waterworks Road. Harry Wilson was the bookie. I had to run across there with the bets that my father had collected and he would pay me threepence.

John Reynolds

One Step Above the Tea Boy

I worked at Collier's and I started off in the general office. It was a three storey building and it had a warehouse attached. I had a letter of introduction from Mr Hughes who was my headmaster. I had to take it to Mr Holbrook and they gave me a job, which was about one step higher than the tea boy! We did a lot of our own advertising and I had to collect the mail. We had four mails a day then. We had an addressograph and it was my job to go though and stamp all those envelopes that was going to have some kind of advert inside. I worked there for seven years before the war broke out. When I got back after the war I went back to Collier's. That was the law, they had to keep your job and you had to have a good reason for not going back. Collier's were Cloth Factors. The mills made the cloth, but we supplied the cloth to tailors and outfitters. We had bunches of sample fabrics with roughly thirty patterns to a bunch.

Tom Hill

"STOCK CARRIED"

WE do not 'bet' although every bunch is 'backed' with stock, and for our Stock, there is no 'better'!

Illustration from an advertising booklet for S. Collier & Co., cloth factors.

Advertisement for a sale at A. Taylors of Church Walk, 1910.

An Apprentice in Millinery

I went straight from school into an apprenticeship in millinery and gowns at Waterfield's in Roundstone Street. I did two years there and then I went from there to millinery and gowns and coats at Butcher's, which is now by the left side of the Post Office. I was there until three of us got put off and I was out unemployed for about two months. I got a job at Miss Bellinger's at Church Street and I was doing millinery again. She sold the property and I was asked to step down or go to work for her husband in Bradford, who was a tailor. I went to Bradford and was there for three years until about 1943.

When I went out to work first of all I earned three and six a week, my mother took the half crown and gave me back the shilling, then the next year I got five shillings, the next raise I had was seven and six. Then my mother passed away and I had to look for something totally different, so I went across to Mr Butcher and I stood up there as bold as brass, and he said how much did I think I ought to earn a week and I said fifteen shillings a week please. I got it and commission on what I sold, but I was the fourth person to be called forward after the other three were serving, so I didn't get very much commission. Miss Bellinger's was just millinery and scarves and hat pins and that kind of thing. I can remember one time, hats were just 2/11, 3/11 and 4/11 at Miss Bellinger's shop, but she took about £60 one Easter Saturday. I used to work from half past eight in a morning till seven o' clock at night, sewing all day. Wednesday afternoons I had a half day. It was hard going.
Enid Hill

The Court Hall Café

For a time I worked at the Court Hall Café. That was the centre of catering in Trowbridge. Miss Burnley was the manageress and I was under manageress. We had the monopoly for catering in Trowbridge and around. We used to do banquets, weddings, the lot. We had dances and balls. In the foyer were small tables with little chairs round and you could have coffee, the back room you could sit and have coffee and be waited on. That was in the days when

40

waitresses wore black with proper aprons with a big bow and you had your white napkin. I remember we did a banquet in the Town Hall for the Wiltshire Times. It was hard work, but we enjoyed it. Not much pay, 1/6 an hour, but the comradeship of the waitresses and that, they were all your friends.

Joyce Hunt

Slaughterhouse Work

I remember our mother looked through the Wiltshire Times and she said, 'Here's a good job for you, good money' and I said, 'What's that?' and she said, 'They want someone to go and help in the slaughterhouse down Court Street'. I was only fourteen. I said, 'How much is it a week?' and she said, 'Thirty bob'. I thought that sounded good, so I went into Ernie Cleveland's shop and he gave me the job on the spot. It was like that in those days, you could get the sack on Friday, you'd be re-employed by Monday.

Well I'd never even been in a slaughter house in my life and I walked in and there were all these great big sides of beef hanging up. They were pulling them up on a pulley, so that the chaps that were taking them could get their shoulder under them. Then they'd let the thing down and they'd carry them away and load them into the lorry. Ernie Cleveland said to me, 'Come on my son, get your kit on' I thought, 'What the blooming hell is he on about?' I didn't have any kit, did I! So they fitted me out with a pair of wellingtons and a rubber apron and I went home covered with blood and muck. I didn't think I could stick it, and our Mam said, 'Stick with it, you might get to like it' and after about a fortnight I'd got used to it and quite liked it. We killed sheep and pigs in Ernie

Dorothy Walton's father, James Avons, working on the railway line near Westbury, *c.* 1931.

Max Connor photographed while working as a conductor with the Western National Bus Company, 1951.

Cleveland's slaughterhouse, that was a bit further down, and all the beef, that was done at the Co-op slaughterhouse. During the war it was all taken over by the Ministry of Food, Ernie Cleveland had the contract there. Sometimes they'd come straight to us from the cattle market and sometimes come up from the railway station, sometimes from other markets by road. I used to have to go up the station and wait for the train, sometimes the animals were already there in pens. Two or three of us would drive them down to the slaughterhouse. If we were full up at the slaughterhouse, we'd have to drive them through the town to Ernie Clevedon's farm, down Green Lane. On the Sunday, ready for Monday, believe it or not, we'd have to drive them back. I'd be in my Sunday best and all. We'd drive them back through the town and they'd get in peoples' gardens, trample every thing. Up West Ashton Road, along Polebarn, turn left and along in front of the Town Hall and through to the yard. Splodging all over the road and all! Some of the cows seemed to know what was happening and on occasions one would go a bit berserk. We used to go in the pen, put a rope around their neck and then the rope went through a big ring on the wall. I'd be on the end of the rope. Once you got the animals head onto that ring I had to secure the rope. One day we had a bull in there and he was doing every thing to get away. The rope broke and he went through the door, up the top of the yard and out behind the Woolpack. Up a little lane where there were some cottages. We couldn't get any where near it. I got on my bicycle and went up to the Halve. All the American servicemen were up there. I went into this building and there was this American officer sat at this desk. I told him about this bull that had escaped and he came up and shot it. We had to put ropes on it and drag it all the way back along to the yard.

Max Connor

Our Little Wiltshire Girl

I was telephonist for a time. Behind the Court Hall Café, there was the Co-op Hall and on the left there was a row of cottages. During the war, the second house from the bottom was the telephone exchange. Nobody knew it. I did all my exams on the telephony with the GPO, someone came up from Bristol and put you all through it. You made friends over the telephone. They used to say, 'Here's our little Wiltshire girl.' They knew you by your accent! There used to be about eight girls all in a row, with the board with all these thousands of black holes. No numbers and you had to test them. Everywhere had a code like Bournemouth might be Bth, and you had to know all of them. You had sets around your chest with your mouth sets. You used to have the telephone boxes where you put your money in and the lights would flash on the board and you used to have to cut in and say, 'Excuse me, your time is up. Do you require extra time? Would you please insert such and such'. Apart from that, you had pads with a pencil and you had to record every call that came in and you had a girl sat at a desk sorting them all out. What category they went in. I expect that was what the bills were made up from.

Joyce Hunt

No Fun for the Conductor

They started out with most of the buses single deckers and then they came to double deckers. When I was conducting in the fifties it was a nightmare. The buses were frequent, hourly buses to Chippenham, Saturdays more frequent than that. Nine times out of ten it was always a standing load. We had the old belt punch and a rack full of tickets. You could leave Trowbridge

Town Hall, which is where all the buses were. You might have up to half a dozen buses there and queues and queues of people. I used to come out with my ticket machine and get on the bus and I used to look at the people and I'd count along, you were only allowed eight standing and you used to have to tell however many to get off the bus. They didn't like that, but I had to get them off. Start as fast as possible collecting the fares, by the time you got to Hilperton, you might be half way up the bus if you were lucky. You stopped at the Lion and Fiddle and of course there were passengers who hadn't paid, and if they were upstairs they used to whizz down the stairs and off before you could do anything.

Max Connor

Seasonal Work

Christmas time, my Dad would work plucking turkeys for Garlick's and Church's. From quite an early age I'd go with him. The one I remember most was Church's who had a loft at the back of where Woolworth's are now. We went up rickety steps and ladders to get to it. These turkeys were all stacked in pens up there in this loft. My Dad would sit with a candle, plucking these turkeys. He'd bring one along and give me four to hold and hand them to him. Then he'd go over them with a candle burning the hairs off them. He'd truss them and do the lot. We always had a jolly good Christmas dinner.

John Reynolds

Gordon Mundy, photographed at an evening class at Bath College.

Driving a Horse and Cart

I left school at fourteen and I went to Haden's Engineering in Silver Street, I was making towel rails there. My mother wasn't satisfied and she was always on the lookout for a better job, so the next thing I knew I had an appointment up the *Wiltshire Times* for an apprenticeship. I got that and I was four years apprenticed as a compositer. I was getting on well there and we were going down to the Bath College one night a week. Two or three of my mates, we were all in this apprentice printing in Trowbridge, see, two at Massey's, one at Slugg's.

After the war I was doing high speed telegraphy which was punch typing and it was shift work. I could never get used to shift work, so I wanted a job outside. I went down the railway station and they were advertising at the time. The station manager in charge, said, 'We have a job, have you had anything to do with horses?' So I said, 'No', and he said, 'Would I be interested in learning to drive a horse and cart'. I said, 'I don't mind, I'll have a go like'. I was only in the goods yard for a week and they come after me to go on the horse and cart. So I was trained up on that, taking the goods round town, delivering the goods. The goods come in the goods yard down the railway station and they had four cars and they kept the four horses to deliver the goods round town. The stables for them were on Court Street. You would go in there, eight o' clock of a morning, groom the horses, hitch them up to the cart and then we did take them out, along half past eight ready for nine o' clock when the shops would open.

We used to come out of Court Street to go to the station on a morning and always go along Bythesea Road and that horse, he would slouch along there, but in the evenings I'd get to Palmer Mackays and pick up the cloth. There was a slope up out of there and you'd always have a bit of weight on, but I didn't have to tell him, he ran up there. It was the same when you got to the station. You unloaded your goods into the carriages, and he always knew when he was going back home, five o' clock at night. He'd run along and sometimes you'd have a job holding him back along Bythesea Road. I had one horse and about the end of the first week with him, I thought he must have been up to Trowbridge before, because I was delivering some stuff to Chapmans. You had to go in and get the chap to come out and sign for it and when we got out my horse and cart were missing. You were supposed to chain them up, but most of the time you didn't because they were all right. I thought, 'Oh dear, where's my horse and cart?' I started walking up the road and I got to the stables. The stable yard was open and in the yard there was a wider area where you turned the cart round and backed it into the shed and there he was standing at the bottom, all ready to be backed in. That was only just after dinner and he

Scene at Chapman's mattress factory, Castle Street in the early 1950s. It later became Airsprung.

thought it was time to go home! In the afternoon, you delivered one load of goods and you each had a round, to collect goods to be sent away. I had Palmer Mackays, Colliers at the top of Duke Street, they'd do small bundles of cloth. Kemp and Hewitt, Clarks, Applegates the engineer. Every day there were things to pick up to be sent away. Always bundles of cloth to be taken up to the station.

Gordon Mundy

Egg Collecting for Waldens

I came up from Dorset and I was a farmer's son. I went as a salesman for fertiliser and seeds and that to the farmers, it was only on commission. Then I worked for Waldens, collecting eggs around the farms. That was quite interesting that was, because you met different folk. It wasn't just collecting from farms it was collecting from cottages as well. People always had the odd chicken in the bottom of their gardens and you used to get a tray of two and a half dozen a week from some and you might get seven trays from another. I used to go right round this area in a three tonner and we used to be full. Waldens used to have their egg packing down Canal Road. We used to go in and they used to sort the grades out. If you had a standard one it was stamped with the lion.

Edgar Davis

Absolute Perfection

I had grandparents in Timbrell Street. He worked at Hadens. A lot of the

Staff at the *Wiltshire Times*, Trowbridge, *c. 1952.*

family did, they were all engineers. In those days, if you wanted to be an engineer you had to pay a lot of money for indentures, as they called it. If your father worked there, the eldest son would be able to go free. My grandfather did it, so my Dad went to learn free, then my brother went as well and he didn't have to pay. If you didn't have any connections you had to pay for these indentures. Years ago, the training was very rigid and you had five years of it. Another friend, he was a painter, he said that for the first year you were only allowed to hold the brush and clean the brushes, and then gradually you learnt to mix paints, then eventually you were actually allowed to paint a door. It was absolute perfection.

Grace Marsden

Telegraph Boys

My brother Hector was a telegraph boy in the old post office. He was very smart. There were two or three of them would stand in the entrance to the post office and whistle to all the girls. All smart with their shoes polished, their clothes all brushed up and their hats on. Their uniform with the red stripe down the side – they did look smart. I had his old overcoat when he grew out of it, I thought I was the bee's knees in that.

John Reynolds

From Paper Round to Inspector

I left school at fourteen, 1931 that was. I went delivering papers for Wymans, the book stall on the station. I used to go to Staverton first of all, then I took on the bigger round and went to Hilperton, Steeple Ashton, West Ashton and North Bradley. That was setting off at half six of a morning and get back somewhere about two o'clock in the afternoon. Twas a good cycle round that was. I expect I used to have about two or three hundred papers, I had the panniers on the side of the bike and a big bundle in the front. For a little chap it was quite a big thing really. Then I went and worked on the bookstall at Devizes. Then after I left there I went to the Avon, at Melksham, until the war broke out. In 1942 I left there and went into the navy. After the war, I worked for the engineering factory – HN engineering, which is in St Georges Works, in Trowbridge, where the billiards place is now. They had a big chimney in there. They made valves for all sorts of things – wagons, tankers, ships, you name it, all that sort of thing. They eventually finished up by doing nearly all the nuclear stations. Nuclear valves for submarines, all that sort of thing. I was inspector when I finished there.

Jack Carter

No Job to Come Back To

I was about sixteen and a half when I left school, I suppose, and I learnt

Illustration from the sales brochure of A. Taylor, 1910.

shorthand and typing with Miss Wason, at her house in Wingfield Road. I got a job at the Agriculture Department of the County Hall, which was where the Roundstone Hotel is now. Instead of putting me on as a shorthand typist, they put me on the telephone exchange. I didn't know that I was hard of hearing, but I had an awful job with this telephone exchange. I couldn't get names. Most of the rooms had numbers as well, so if the person phoning in asked to be put through to a number then it was easy. If they asked me to speak to a particular person by name, I had an awful job with it. So after a year I got another job as shorthand typist in the ARP department, in the Health

Department at County Hall. I was there for a year and then I joined the Women's ATS. After the war I didn't have a job to come back to because I'd volunteered. If you waited to be called up they kept your job for you, but because I'd volunteered I didn't have a job at County Hall to come back. I was at a loose end when I came back. Jobs were scarce with all the men coming back as well. Soon after that I met my husband and was married in 1947 and in those days married women didn't have jobs. My husband had Taylor's shop then, his father had died during the early part of the war. The shop never changed. I did work at the shop later on when the children were at school, I started working in the office, working out the prices and checking off the goods as they came in. They had haberdashery and wool, materials, ribbons, stockings and underwear, then jumpers and cardigans and hats upstairs.

Vera Taylor

Work at the Co-op

I left school when I was fourteen and I went to work in the Co-op office in Rodney House, Roundstone Street. I'd learnt shorthand and typing, I used to do the letters for the secretary, Jimmy Wareham. He was a lovely man, ever so nice. When you got some groceries at the Co-op, you were given a little check, then we had all little partitions and had to sort them out and add them up. We had an adding machine, even in those days, at the end of the month and then at the end of six months they knew how much dividend they could get. Of course some people saved every receipt and they would come back and say, 'That isn't right'. The Co-op was a huge concern – it had everything imaginable. My friend worked there and they had a little switchboard of their own it was such a big concern.

Grace Marsden

Responsibilities for a Lad

I left school at fifteen and a half on a Friday and I started work at Sylvester and Macketts on the Monday. I was only office boy, in fact I only stayed there six weeks, because I really wanted to go to County Hall. I was in this little reception office, I had to answer the phone and deal with callers. Mr Mackett had a secretary and he would walk up and down like a barrister dictating and you could hear him out in reception. If he ever asked for me – if he rang up on the phone and asked me for anything, I didn't need to listen to the phone I could just hear him and I would just talk back into the phone. I did like general office work really. Even though I was only an office boy, I was given great responsibility. I had to unlock the building on a morning and lock up at night. The post office was down Wicker Hill and part of my job was to go to the post office in a morning and get all the mail in a huge bag and bring it back to Sylvester and Mackett's and they would

County Hall after fire damaged the roof in 1958.

Case's butchers shop on Mortimer Street, c. 1960.

open it. The secretaries would do the letters and I'd have to dash to the post office at the end of the day to get them in and I wouldn't get off until about half past six. I had to close up the office, lock up the strong room and put the keys away, and this was all within a week or two of leaving school. I was on the books at the Employment Exchange and they said there was a job going at County Hall, would you like to try for it. So I went to County Hall and I had an interview and got a job in the surveyors office. You were just called by your surname in those days – it was Jones. No one was called by their Christian names and you called those above you Mr So-and-so. County Hall in those days was like something out of the Victorian age, so old fashioned. They had never changed things – about

one phone per office and if there was a call from Wilton, it was a wonderful event and all the old boys would queue up at the phone. I used to work every other Saturday. They had a funny bell system then, the County Surveyor and the Deputy County Surveyor had this wonderful system like the old fashioned hotel systems. If they'd ring a bell, a disk would come down in your room and there was a different disk for different people. One disk for the boss of the office, two disks for the second one, three disks for the junior and so on in each room. My job at half past twelve on a Saturday was to go round and make sure all the windows in the offices were shut, so after twelve o' clock I'd set off round the offices. I went into the County Surveyor's room, this one time and he had this table and this massive thing with all these levers and buttons and I couldn't resist it. I pressed something and all the bells went and as I came out of the office I was nearly knocked down – all the old stagers were coming, 'What's he want at this time of morning?', all muttering away.

Stanley Jones

Working at Cases

Later on I went to Cases, that's where I learnt the butchers trade. I went there and saw Mr Case and he asked if I'd done anything like it before and I said no, but I was a farmer's son and he looked at me and said, 'You'll be alright, you can have the job as a salesman, but you got to make sure you know what your talking about, so I'm going to give you three weeks or a month in the factory.' So I had to see all the work in the factory and then he said I had to go into the shop. You had white overalls. I must admit that everything was clean, you were shown how to scrub the tables, the benches – well they used to call them blocks in them days. You used to cut up the meat on them. You had a stack of cloths to wipe down every time you did a job, everything clean before you started another one. Not everywhere was as clean as that, but even in the factory and that, it all had to be spotlessly clean. Mr Case had an office up above and if he ever came down it had to be spotless. Even when you'd killed the pigs and that it all had to be hosed down. You had to serve in the shop as well, and once you done that, he said, 'You can go out on the road'. Mr Case said that I sold more in

the first twelve months, than anybody had sold for a long time. They used to have all the pig fat – the lard – and the cellar was nearly full of that, and I near emptied that. In the shop there was bacon in one end and beef in the other. Marble slabs with glass at the front and they had trays with all the things on and you used to have to pull the trays out. What the customer wanted you had to give them.

Edgar Davis

A Daily Help

When I left school, I had to go out to work, 'cause my mother couldn't keep us. I went as a daily help to Miss Bennett. She used to be a missionary for the parish church, in Uganda. I worked up there for her for 4/- a week, from eight till six, and eight till two on Sundays. She lived in those houses on the Down, almost opposite the Canal Road. Her sister had arthritis and she was in an invalid chair and I used to have to go and look after her all day. I worked there for a month and then she gave me an extra shilling. Out in the kitchen she had a little oil stove and you had to light it. She had a big dog and when I'd lit the stove I had to take the dog out. This particular day, when I got back, well you never seen nothing like it in all your life. The stove had smoked and it were black everywhere. I'd got the oil too high. All the cobwebs were black. Well, I've got a bit of a temper and I wouldn't ever be put upon and she jawed me and that and I got me bike and I went home. My Mother said, "You're not staying home'

John Almond delivering for the Modeluxe Laundry in the late 1950s.

and she marched I back see and I had to say I was sorry. But I had to clean it all up.

Alice Smart

The Model Laundry

My husband worked at the Model Laundry for twenty years. He started there as a stoker, then he went into the wash room and then onto the vans. Then he was manager of the shop on the barracks for the Americans and they had a dry cleaning shop there and my husband used to have to go there and collect and different things.

Lilian Almond

My First Job

I was ready for work and an opportunity opened for me with James Ladd. His business was a builder's merchants. My father worked there as a sort of traveller-cum-go-between with the different reps who'd come and call. James Ladd, who had founded the company, had said to my father, 'If you think Lynda is ready to leave her course, I could do with somebody who is reliable and able to write cheques and be clear and neat and tidy. There's a lot of secretarial type work that we need to have somebody in the office for.' Although they had other people doing other jobs, there was nobody actually acting in a personal sort of way to him. He thought it would relieve him of having to do some of those more menial tasks.

Lynda Bosworth

Roberts' shop on the corner of Mortimer Street and Bythesea Road, around the turn of the century.

Pharmacist at Aplin's

My father was called Ernest John Sykes and he was from Bath and had trained as a pharmacist there. He worked in Aplin's when he came to Trowbridge before the First World War. I was there many times when I was small. There was a side door that I used to go in and I was often upstairs with him. The shop had all these drawers containing things and all the lovely bottles with the mauve and the green in. Of course in those days they had to make up all the tablets up on the premises and all the medicines and that. He used the pestle and mortar. I remember seeing him many times. They would get the prescription from the doctor and he would have to make it up from the different things.

Mary Martin

Changes at Knee's

When my grandfather started the business, it was where Foster's was on the end of Church Walk, he used to sell anything he could buy. It was a little tiny place and he was there from 1879. He was a very energetic little man, extraordinarily different from his brothers and sisters. He built up a most wonderful business with the big houses that were still all here. When I first turned up here, it was at the end of the big families, they were all going broke I suppose. We were always in trouble with money, because although they were wonderful customers, they never used to pay the bill until they died or near enough! It didn't matter what you

Ernest John Sykes was pharmacist at Aplin's for many years.

A Posh Photographer

Houlton's had a staff of about fifteen working for them in days gone by. I had my photo taken to send to my husband, the first Christmas he was away. I was twenty one. Houlton's was a posh photographer. Very nice people, two brothers. They had all the picture frames to choose from for when you had a picture taken. You could get films and cameras in there, they did mounting and that kind of thing. Behind was the studio and the workshop where all the girls used to work.

Enid Hill

charged them, so of course we charged them a lot of money. We used to go into the house and change all the curtains and put up the summer curtains and take all the copper saucepans away while the family were taking a holiday and tin the insides. We used to do the whole thing, keep the whole house immaculate and all together. When I came over not only was it very difficult to get any money out of them, but they were starting to close down. We had all these staff and we were lucky enough to get the same kind of job doing the furnishings for the ships at Avonmouth. The corner shop – now the travel agent, we had that as a sort of introduction to the building as it were. We used to take the money there and we had a little office behind. My grandfather built that and he was going to live in the flat above. There was a little staircase used to go up at the back there. Then he never lived there, he bought Rosebank instead. We used to use it as various showrooms.

Noel Knee

Gunstone's Bakery

Just between the two entrances to the Tabernacle Church there was a little shop – a bakers – and Mrs Gunstone ran that with her husband. He only had one arm. She always used to open up and bake hot cross buns and that was a Good Friday ritual to go down to Mrs Gunstone's shop and get fresh baked hot cross buns. They ran this little shop for years.

Stanley Jones

Fred Whitmarsh's boot and shoe shop in Church Walk.

Whitmarsh's Boots and Shoes

My grandfather started with the shop and then my father took it over and we were there, in Church Walk until 1960, when my father died. My grandfather was a jeweller, but my father had a boot and shoe shop. He was down Fore Street, I think first and then when my grandfather died, my father moved into the shop in Church Walk. They were open long hours. They opened at 9 every day and they were open till 6 on Mondays and Tuesdays, till 1 o'clock on Wednesdays – it were a half day always. Thursday I think it was open till 7, Friday till 8 and Saturday till 9. People started getting paid towards the end of the week. In the early days, my father used to do repairs as well, so when he finished he had to go up and start repairs. We had a room at the top called the linen room and he had machinery up there to make stuff and do repairs.

Jessie Whitmarsh

Shopping for Ball Gowns

When we were older, we went to the balls at the Town Hall. There were a lot of balls then. We probably got our dresses from Bath. Of course in those days you could take things home on approval, try them on and could leave them a couple of weeks, then take them back again. There was no trouble about that. We would go to Jolly's quite a lot. It was a really good shop, quality things then. My mother used to get her hats there and they'd come in a cardboard hat box. She used to take

The Three Horseshoes Inn on Mortimer Street.

them back if she didn't like them. We used to get things from Fear Hills. That was quite a good shop then.

Anne Mackay

Rose's Bakery

The nearest shop to us in Bond Street was Rose's Bakery which was just on the corner and we would go up and buy tuppeny buns, currant buns or a loaf of bread. We used to always try to choose a crusty one and get the little bits off the top before you got home. It would be wrapped in one piece of tissue paper, so it wouldn't be very difficult to pick the corner.

Lynda Bosworth

Getting the Divvy

At the Co-op when you went into the shop and bought anything you had to give your divvy number, so they kept a record on the till receipts. You got your divvy every six months and you had to go to the Co-op offices at Rodney House to claim it. There was a little narrow street, Thomas Street, and there was a general shop – groceries, drinks and that. The lady what ran it, she was so plump, she used to sit behind the counter and you had to more or less help yourself. She had someone else there occasionally. We used to go to the cobblers and have our shoes mended. There was one down at Church Walk – Whitmarsh, a shoe shop, but he did repairs as well. We got most of our shoes there. Mother would take us there. He

was a lovely person, very kind and very obliging.

Dorothy Walton

The Sweet Factory

This place next to St Thomas' was a sweet factory. The old chap who worked there was called Thickit and you could watch them making all the sweets. Rosebuds – they were the favourite, red and white hard sweets they were. We went for bulls eyes mainly. Mint shrimps, the red and white ones that was another one. Bulls eyes seemed to last longer.

Gordon Mundy

Shops on Mortimer Street

On Mortimer Street you started off with the Three Horseshoes, number 1 Mortimer Street. You had Sally Ducks – she used to sell all sorts in there at No. 4 Mortimer Street, I was born next door to that at No. 3. Then you had Trollope's shop which was on the corner with Bythesea Road. On the opposite corner of Bythesea Road was Roberts, Consul Roberts as we called him. He used to sell all sorts of groceries, vegetables, paraffin, eggs – you name it. Almost adjoining him was Cases the bacon purveyors. There was another shop – I can't think of the name of that one, a sweet shop cum cakes as well. There was a shoe repairer, there was Marshman's – also greengrocers cum vegetable person, a hairdresser, another boot repairer Alan

Mortimer and then Spender's the fish shop. Then over the bridge was the Greyhound pub, which is still there. You had the Co-op shop was put there later on. It wasn't there originally. Then there was another little sort of sweet shop cum biscuits and right on the corner of Mortimer Street before you break into Newtown, there was Sleightholme's cycle factory. On the left hand side going up there was only the Lamb public House and then just all cottages and cul-de-sacs all the way up.

Jack Carter

A Big Store

Fear Hills was a big store. They had three floors – the ground floor they had haberdashery and underwear and things, on the next floor, further back – curtain materials and that and then up a few more steps they had outer wear and hats, dresses and suits. When I was young we bought things there, although we didn't have much money in those days.

Vera Taylor

Groceries Delivered

Mum used to have all her groceries delivered from the Co-op which was at the bottom of Gloucester Road. She would make a list out at the weekend and one of us would have to drop it off on Monday morning on our way to school through the little door. All the groceries would be delivered on the Monday afternoon and when we came in from school, there were all these groceries we had to help put away.

Lynda Bosworth

Postcard view of Fore Street, sent in 1906. Note the drinking fountain on the left.

A view of Castle Street, Trowbridge. Note the tall building at the top of the hill on the right, which was the Victoria Institute.

Sweets on Ration

Now the sweetshops – the one I really remember was Henry Overton's, that was our sweetshop. You'd go up there and you'd get the sherbet dips, and the penny sweets and lollipops and things like that. There was another shop in Church Walk – Jenkins I think it was, that was another old fashioned sweet shop. You could go in there, but it was wartime and sweets were rationed. You had them on coupons. What we used to do, from about September onwards, we didn't have a sweet at all. We used to save up all the coupons, so that we could have chocolates and sweets at Christmastime. I remember there were some sweets that you could still buy that were not rationed, like mints and that type of thing. There was a sweet factory in Roundstone Street, behind what is now the factory shop. It was called Wilkins. They had the shop – the Dinkie – a wonderful shop, where there was this delightful lady and we used to go in there and get our sweets. It had a wonderful atmosphere in there. You could almost smell the sweets, they were all home made. I remember this lady, when she was serving, she would always be chewing, she always had a sweet in her mouth.

Stanley Jones

Shopping with a Pram

The town centre was quite busy, there were no supermarkets. The busiest shop was always the International Stores, which was on the corner opposite the Town Hall. That was always packed, because it was the

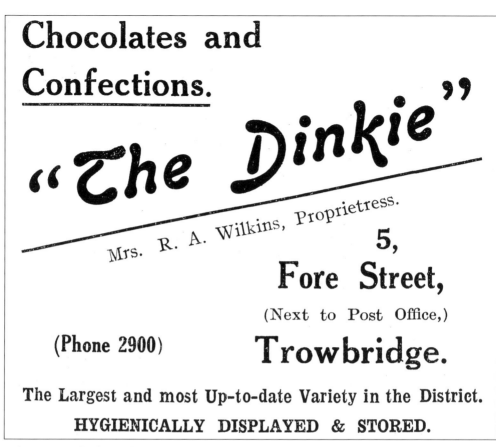

Chocolates and Confections.

"The Dinkie"

Mrs. R. A. Wilkins, Proprietress.

5,
Fore Street,

(Next to Post Office,)

(Phone 2900)

Trowbridge.

The Largest and most Up-to-date Variety in the District.
HYGIENICALLY DISPLAYED & STORED.

Advertisement for the Dinkie in a 1949 directory.

only self service store in the town. It was very tiny and you sort of shuffled round with your basket, filling it up and getting to the other end. But of course you shopped much more often than you do now. A lot of people wouldn't have had a fridge and you didn't have a freezer, so you had to shop two or three times a week. I used to walk from Horse Road into town, do my shopping and walk all the way back again, with a pram once I had the children, because of course you couldn't take the pram on the bus. The shopping – I had a pram basket which I always filled and some of it was pushed on a sort of tray underneath the pram and the rest was

hung on handles. You never took your child into a shop, you always left them outside, with all the lovely Mums and Grans gathered round talking and smiling at the child. I can remember once going into the greengrocers and the pram was so laden down, that when I looked out the pram had virtually tipped up, with the children slipped down. They didn't come to any harm. I rushed outside and picked it all up again.

Marion Dutch

Corner Shops

On Dursley Road there was a shop called Porters, just by the footbridge, it was just there and there was another one further up called Vince's I think. There were a lot of small shops. It was all little old corner shops, much more convenient than it is today.

Grace Marsden

A Penn'orth of Sweets

The Church Walk was thriving in those days, because the people who brought their children to school and met them afterwards, used to shop and cut through there. It was always a very busy and thriving little area. I think there was a sweet shop, a tiny little shop, next to where the Co-op used to be in Church Street. The children used to pop across and get their penn'orth or tuppence of sweets before they came to school in the mornings.

Marion Dutch

The Drum

All the odds and ends we bought in Taylors and you could even go in and buy one button if you wanted to. There were an awful lot of people making sweets in Trowbridge. There was one in Church Walk. They only made in their kitchen, and most of the things what they made were great big things – humbugs, and you bought them separately. I don't know whether they were a farthing each or something. On one side of my father's shop was Wards,

View of Church Walk, probably in the 1930s.

a newsagent selling papers, and on the other side it were Purnells, a mans outfitters. He made the suits there. The Post office was down the Parade, near Hardings. There was a big house up Duke street. If you went up there, near the Wiltshire Times there was an opening where you could go through and you come out by the fish shop, down on Roundstone Street. It was called the Drum. When I was a child you used to go up there and run through.

Jessie Whitmarsh

Wiltshire and Cockney

Henry Overtons shop our children used to like at the time when we lived up Middle Lane. The children used to walk down Middle Lane and I used to give them a halfpenny a day and they would get their sweets. Mr Overton used to say he loved to listen to my children talk because they were a cross between Wiltshire and cockney. They used to buy chocolate mints, bulls eyes and snowballs, penny bars of chocolate in the silver foil. All the sweets were in jars on show around the shop. They used to have a piece of paper and they used to roll it into a cone and twist the bottom and put the sweets into that. If they spent more than tuppence, they had it in a white paper bag.

Lilian Almond

Gladys Earl pictured outside Earl's Hardware shop in Church Street, 1958. The girl is Christine Reynolds, whose parents were the caretakers of nearby Parochial School.

Shopping at the Co-op

We used to get our shopping in two parts – we used to go to the Co-op for the big shop. They used to have late night opening – till about 7, my mother always used to go down and do our weeks shopping between 6 and 7 at the Co-op, Friday evening. They had all different counters for every thing – bakery, bacon, sugar and everything. The butchers was next door. The old fashioned grocers used to deliver, the boy would come down with it on his big old fashioned bike.

Stanley Jones

Late Night Shopping

Saturday nights were busy 'cause the shops didn't close till 8 o'clock. A lot of people didn't used to go to do their shopping till that time. Woolworths used to get packed out. They used to have a garage just down below Woolworths one time. That was very awkward 'cause the cars were in and out. There used to be fruit and veg shops up at Roundstone Street and Pitts has always been there. There was a music shop higher up.

Lilly Pickett

The Market Yard

I remember we got our first dog from the market. Below the indoor market there were a few steps going down to the market yard and on your right there were chickens and rabbits and that and

Fred Hardiman's Woodworker Supply Stores in Newtown in 1934. Les Hardiman, Fred's younger brother, stands outside.

any dogs, they tied them up to a post in that area. There was a black retriever cross and we went and looked and then later when I got home from school, Mum had bought it for five shillings. It was there in our back yard. It was about six months old. We called him Nip. You could buy anything in the market in those days. Thinking of the cattle market, when I was in my teens, they used to drive the cattle through the streets of the town and one time some young cows got in the churchyard and the verger had to chase them out and along back to the market. But I remember watching from my window in Church Walk. Farmer Whitley used to work down the cattle market getting them into the pens and that for the auctioneer. He always wore a farmer's smock. In the market hall there was a man sold cheap china plates and if no-one bought them, he just threw them down and broke them. I used to love to stand watching. They sold secondhand clothes, materials and carpets and there was a decent china stall as well.

Jessie Whitmarsh

With Christmas Greetings
and Best Wishes for the
New Year

From

The President of the

Chamber of Commerce.

B. B. Garlick,
Cockhill House,
Trowbridge.   Dec., 1927.

Trowbridge and District Chamber of Commerce Christmas card sent in 1927.

A gentleman rides his penny farthing bicycle around the old Market Yard.

CHAPTER 5

Entertainment and sport

Members of Bethesda Junior church dressed for the carnival, probably just before the First World War.

Magic Lanterns

Harold Baker lived in Broad Street. He had a chicken house at the back of their house and we used to pay him cigarette cards to go in and see his magic lantern show. For a couple of cigarette cards we'd sit for ten minutes or so looking at the magic lantern and then he would bring out cold tea as a drink. No sugar and no milk, just cold tea.

John Reynolds

Social Club at the Mill

We had what they did call a little social club at the mill. We used to have a skittle alley and all. You'd pay so much a week. We used to have dances at the Co-op hall, which was down a little lane at the side of the Woolpack. We used to pay sixpence to go to these dances down there and we used to have outings, we used to go to Weston. We had good times.

Lilly Pickett

The Police Sports

The thing that always sticks in my mind with the County Ground, once a year the Police Sports were always held there. That was a good day out. They had the marquees, everything. All the county police were represented there. We had a Sgt Shears did chase us, when we were playing football in the street and he was the fastest and we would always go up there on sports day

and cheer him on in the hundred yards.

Gordon Mundy

Co-op Sports Day

The Co-op held a sports at the back of their office there in Roundstone Street. I remember jumping against a very tall lad, whose father kept a radio shop down on Wicker Hill, Jimmy James. We were in the finals and I beat him in the high jump. I got a shoe box as a prize with a polishing brush, a blacking brush and a tin of Pelaw polish that the Co-op used to make. My parents were there and very proud of me.

John Reynolds

Carnival Ball

In the *Wiltshire Times*, when it was coming up to Carnival time, you had girls who had put their names down for Carnival Queen. The whole town could vote through the *Wiltshire Times*. You had to vote for who you thought were the seven best from the picture page. They chose one for queen and six for her attendants. You also had the butterfly queen, the little girl. On the Friday night there was the Carnival Ball at the Town Hall. They used to put this huge red carpet outside from the pavement's edge and everybody used to arrive in these wonderful cars on the night in their lovely gowns. All the shop windows were dressed for carnival week, like Fear Hills, Waterfields, they all had their lovely ball gowns in the

An early carnival procession passes down Wicker Hill, probably before 1910.

TOWN HALL, TROWBRIDGE.

THURSDAY, SEPTEMBER 1st. 1932, AT 7 P.M.

·ENTHRONEMENT of the
QUEEN OF CARNIVAL and CARNIVAL PRINCESS

◈ PROGRAMME ◈

COMMUNITY SINGING (conducted by Mr. Wallis Elloway).

MR. SIDNEY SMITH (Chairman, Trowbridge U.D.C.) on behalf of the Town and District will invite Major E. A. Mackay, T.D., as representing the Trowbridge Woollen Cloth Industry, to Preside.

MAJOR MACKAY will open the sealed envelope and Announce the Name of the Queen.

MRS. H. LOVELL HEWITT, assisted by Master Donald Mackay, as Page of Honour, will Crown and Enthrone the Queen.

LAST YEAR'S CARNIVAL QUEEN (Miss E. Wheeler) will offer Congratulations to her Successor and Present her with a Bouquet.

MAJOR MACKAY will read and hand to the Queen a Congratulatory Address, together with a Key with which to open the hearts of her Subjects.

MR. ALBERT LESTER will read Her Majesty's Reply, which will be handed to Major Mackay.

MRS. H. LOVELL HEWITT will Invest the Maids of Honour with their Badges of Office.

THE CARNIVAL PRINCESS will then be Escorted to the Platform, Welcomed, Crowned, and Enthroned, by Mrs. H. Lovell Hewitt. Miss Wheeler will hand her a Wand of Office.

MR. A. G. PONTING will Propose a Vote of Thanks to the Queen, the Princess, the Maids of Honour, and all who entered the Competitions.

MR. J. S. JAMES (President of the Chamber of Commerce) will Second the Vote of Thanks.

THE QUEEN and THE PRINCESS will Respond.

MR. F. A. SLUGG, on behalf of the Committee, will Propose a Vote of Thanks to Mrs. H. Lovell Hewitt and Major E. A. Mackay.

MR. F. H. BLAIR (Chairman of the Committee) will Second the Motion.

GOD SAVE THE KING.

THE QUEEN, PRINCESS, and MAIDS OF HONOUR will afterwards appear on the Town Hall Balcony.

E. LANSDOWN & SONS, TROWBRIDGE

Programme for the enthronement of the Carnival Queen in 1932.

windows. I was about thirteen or fourteen and I was fascinated to see these lovely sights of the gowns and everything. That was where a lot of trade came from, because all the shops were dressed for the occasion. Even things like Brown's fish shop had a wonderful display.

Enid Hill

Trowbridge Carnival

The park wasn't that different, with the seats at the top there and the tennis courts, croquet and the wooden band stand. We used to have a lot of concerts there – like the Bath Spa Band

would come up and there was the Devizes Silver Band, Eddington had one and they used to go in the carnivals. They had all the engines and that down in the Market Yard. There was roundabouts, the horses that went up and down and the chairoplanes. Lots of stalls, skittles, throwing a dart and that and you'd win a doll or something.

Alice Smart

Albert Taylor

I can remember possibly the last carnival before the war, the park used to be lit up – all the trees by the bandstand and

The Clive Downer's Dance Orchestra, one of many bands that played at the Town Hall in the 1930s.

Mr Frank Connor and the British Legion Boys Bugle Band.

all around the tennis courts and the elms, they used to have all coloured lights on those trees. The old gent that used to lead the procession, he was the figurehead of the town then – a chap called Albert Taylor. He was the manager at Fosters and used to be the organiser of the carnival. He was always marching at the head of the procession and whenever you saw the procession, there was the Fire Brigade and then Albert Taylor marching along in front.

Stanley Jones

Bugle Band

As a boy my father had been in the Boys Brigade, a drummer boy he was by the time he was twelve and then a bugler. After the war there was some kind of dispute between the leaders of the band and my dad formed his own band, called the British Legion Boys Bugle Band. A lot of the lads went with him. They did all sorts of promotional things, like when they showed the film Desert Victory at the Gaumont, they were there outside with the band. War Weapons week, Spitfire Week. When they had all these different things, my father would turn out sometimes on his own, sometimes with others. During the different appeals they had a barometer outside the Town Hall, and Dad used to be up on the balcony and there would be hundreds of people there, and he'd play his bugle before the announcement of the new total. The band used to play all over the place. They always played in the carnival procession.

Max Connor

70

Carnival Queen

I was lucky enough to be chosen as the last Trowbridge and District Hospital Carnival Queen in 1939. I didn't do all my reign, because the war broke out. I was nearly seventeen. There were about forty entries and you went to the Town Hall. The judging was very thorough. You had to walk, to sit down and you had to read. They came and talked to you. It was quite an ordeal. From the forty it came down to five. The five of us went to Houltons and had our photographs taken and they were displayed in the shop window. Before the final night of choosing the queen, you had to go in a small room at the Town Hall and you were vetted again. On the actual night, you went into the Town Hall and you were spoken to and then you walked up the stairs and you were put in the front row and the concert began. Then after the announcement of the queen, I cried – I couldn't help it! You had to make a speech to the Trowbridge people at the concert and then you came out on the balcony with the spotlight, with your maids of honour. It was a wonderful time. My dress was from Fear Hills, a beautiful white gown and the queen's cloak was blue velvet with a white rabbit fur collar. Then you had the sash with the Trowbridge coat of arms round you. The crown was beautiful with crystal beads. Lady Sybil Phipps lent me her fan of ostrich feathers, so instead of me carrying a bouquet, I carried her fan. You had to go to Houltons again. Old Mr Houlton, he was a wonderful photographer and he posed you and got the folds just so and everything. My big photograph cost me eight guineas, which was a lot of money then. You had it displayed in Houltons window with the four maids of honour.

Carnival Queen Joyce Hanham with her attendants in 1939. From left to right: Grace Foyle, Pamela Davis, Joyce Hanham, -?-, Dorothy Grimshaw, Daisy May.

We had a most beautiful float for the carnival. It was huge and golden. My throne was at the back and the four maids of honour sat at either side. A beautiful setting it was.

Joyce Hunt

Lighting up the Park

All the way round the park, in the shrubs and under the trees, they used to have these like little stained glass jars, like Oxo jars on strings hanging from the trees. All the youngsters used to get their candles and have to drop them in, then they'd go round and light them. They used to do that every day of the carnival. All these coloured jars, it looked beautiful.

Jack Carter

So Many things to See

After the war, the carnivals started again in 1948. The carnival used to be on from Wednesday right through to Saturday, but the two big days were Wednesday and Saturday. The Market Yard was for Jennings Fair and they used to put a fence across the park from the bowling green right across, and you had to pay to go in that part of the park. Us children had to pay 6d, I think. They would have people at the different entrances – by the Town Hall, Polebarn and from the Market Yard. We'd go in there all the afternoon and the great thing was that if you had your hand stamped you didn't have to pay in the evening. There used to be a big entertainment in the afternoon, probably a pipe band, children's sports and everything and the fair was open alongside of it. On Wednesday, the

Usher's Brewery winning tableaux in the 1936 Trowbridge Carnival.

Dagenham Girls band or whoever, would always be met at the station at about 11 o'clock and they would march up through the town to be welcomed and all us kids would go along the side of them. On the afternoon you'd have the local dignitaries, the Carnival Queen and princess and the band and they would go along Bythesea Road to the Park to open the afternoon proceedings. In the evening it would all start again. Wednesday evening they would have like a carnival procession, all sorts of tableaux and instead of everybody going away at the end like they do now, everybody went to the park. All the afternoon performances would be repeated again and the fair going in the old market yard, with the old fashioned side shows, mini circuses and that and it ended up about 9 o' clock with a huge firework display right at the Polebarn Road end. That end of the lawn was cordoned off for the firework display. They reckoned there were about five thousand people watching that. If you weren't in the park early, I remember we watched it from right back at the War Memorial. The whole lawn was completely solid with people. They repeated this on Saturday as well. I think the Saturday afternoon was the children's fancy dress, like they do now and it was usually the Dagenham Girl Pipers there. The whole town was absolutely solid with people. It used to go on to quite late at night. It was marvellous really.

Stanley Jones

The Lantern Procession

They used to have the lantern processions as well in carnival week. We'd get these little paper lanterns that you'd pull up and a candle would go in and we used to go round and my mother used to push the pram with me in. I remember her pushing me, and we used to go all around the town and then disperse in the park. You'd get in the park free, see if you had a lantern. Anybody could walk in the lantern procession – the more the better, as long as you got a lantern you could march. We always liked to march behind the band, the first band. I took my daughter as well, I used to push the pushchair and she did have her lantern. Those with nice lanterns used to get put first. We had a Chinese one, not paper, but sort of silky, my husband had got them from somewhere.

Lilly Pickett

The Modeluxe Laundry carnival entry of the early 1960s. John Almond is at the far back right.

All the Bands

Most of the carnival stalls used to be actually in the park, the coconut shies and the darts, all that sort of thing and the roundabouts used to be in the market yard where all the cattle pens were. It was amazing really to see how they fitted it all in. They had the big wheels and the horses and the chairoplanes, all sorts of things in there. All the stalls in there they belonged to Jennings and they were the mainstay of it and they used to pay so much to the carnival committee for the use of it. The money raised always went to the hospital, because it was the hospital carnival, they used to call it the Trowbridge and District Hospital Carnival. I presume that was how it started, to raise funds for the hospital, which was at the Halve then. Bands were plentiful then – Bratton Band, Bath Spa Band, Frome Band, Melksham Town Band, Trowbridge Town Band – they used to get all these bands to come to the carnival, whereas now you're hard pressed to get a band to come, well then you'd have half a dozen bands.

Jack Carter

The Tin Band

There was an old tin church at the top of the Conigre where they had services every Sunday. It was attached to the parish church and I think they sent a missionary down each Sunday! We used to go there to a boys' club, run by Jim Gorman. I think we had to pay a penny to go to this club. During the evening we might do boxing and play cards, with only Jim to supervise us and half way through the evening, we would get our cup of cocoa and a biscuit perhaps. Jim always took part in the carnival. He had a tin band with all the kids and he would walk in front like the drum major. It was the biggest bunch of rogues in the Conigre – the Tin Band.

John Reynolds

Learning to Swim

I learned to swim at what they call Sandy Bottom. That was the shallow part there along Biss Meadows, you could put your foot down there, further up was Black Ball hatches. That was where the older ones what could swim did go up there. There was bathing sheds just along past where Tesco's is, where the Biss Park is now. I remember going down from Adcroft School, walking down to the bathing sheds for swimming lessons. There was no swimming pool then. We used to swim up in the canal under what they call Clarks bridge. One of my mates he could swim from Clarks bridge down to the next bridge and back again. It wasn't so bad then, it deteriorated during the war with all green slime, though we have swum in the green slime an' all!

Gordon Mundy

Bathing in the Biss

I cycled to Bradford on Avon, because there was no swimming pool here, they had some baths on the right hand

Swimming at Black Ball Hatches in 1931. The Chalke brothers are on the left and Jack Carter and Les Boscombe on the right.

side, where the library is now. We used to go there early morning, several of us and I learnt to swim there. Down the river Biss, they had what you call the hatches. My dad and my brother used to go there in the summer for swimming and that was your bath really. You used to take some soap and that. I didn't – we had a tin bath on Friday nights, but in the summer the boys would go up there, the men could go but not women.

Grace Marsden

The Open Air Pool

We used to walk down to the open air pool quite early on a Sunday morning, about 7 o'clock, half past seven. It was very cold at that time of a morning. It opened at 7 and then they used to close up about 9, I think and open up again later. There were never many people down at that time. It was a nice pool, quite big enough to have a good swim in.

Anne Mackay

Trowbridge Pubs

Pubs – the Crown is still there. Next to the Bethesda Chapel there was the Royal Oak, the Black Swan was always there. The Harp – that's where I met the wife, that was down the Conigre, there was about two or three pubs down there. It's amazing when you think back how many pubs there were in Fore Street. The White Hart, the

View of the Boating Lake in Trowbridge Park, 1939.

New Inn, King's Arms, the George. Used to go there, specially during the war. Quite a popular place that was.

Gordon Mundy

Saturday Night Fights

There were three pubs in the Conigre – the George, the Coach and Horses and the Harp. Further round in Hill Street there was the Kitcheners Arms. There were usually fights on a Saturday night. Even the soldiers and police would walk round in twos there.

John Reynolds

Darts

There used to be good entertainment down the Kitcheners Arms, down the bottom of Back Street, opposite the Billiard Hall. The Elephant and Castle in Castle Street. That was a quaint little old pub. When you played darts, if you went and threw it just a little bit too high, you threw it into the ceiling 'cause it was so low down you see. Oh yes, I had many a dart in their ceiling.

Mavis Burt

The Town Hall

We used to have dancing upstairs at the Town Hall. The large room next to the council chamber, that had a sprung dance floor and it had a place for the band. It had a beautiful wood beam ceiling. We'd had a very expensive kitchen put in up there and I think you could seat four hundred and twenty people. We used to have concerts and the Hunt Ball used to be held there.

Knees did upholstery in those days, we used to decorate the whole hall, put down a beautiful dance floor that cost us an awful lot as a company. It gave a springing effect because it was all in sections. It had carpet underneath. It was a real asset was that place.

Noel Knee

First Time at the Cinema

The first film I saw, my brother took me, I think it was the *Graf Zeppelin*. We always went to the Gaumont on a Saturday morning. Then we'd come out and come up Church Walk and get our Bullseye comic. They had a serial in there – the *Phantom of Curseter Fields*.

We'd read that and in the evenings we'd go out and play it !

Gordon Mundy

First Films at the Cinema

My first memory of going to the pictures, it was the Gaumont, when *Snow White* came out as a new film about 1937. I also remember going to see *Gulliver's Travels*. We also went to the Saturday morning club at Bythesea Road, the Regal. We paid sixpence and it was a huge cinema inside. I remember trying to get in there, later on, to watch the *Dambusters*, when that came out, but we never got there because the queue was through the open space next

A winning darts team from the Lamb public house.

Hula Hoop competition held at the Gaumont cinema, *c.* 1960. Ron Almond is on the left.

to the cinema, right round the back by the railway and back again into Bythesea Road. So we never got in.

Stanley Jones

The Flea Pit

I used to get threepence a week for doing my chores and I used to go to the pictures with my brother in the afternoon. We were always told we had to go in the tuppeny seats, not the penny seats, because it was a flea pit. On a couple of occasions we went in the penny seats and spent the penny on something else.

Enid Hill

Needing an Accumulator

I remember my brother making these crystal sets and then he graduated to a three valve set and you had what you called an accumulator. You had to take it somewhere and they would get it charged up and just when you wanted to listen to something the accumulator would go dead. Unless you had a spare, but it wasn't run off electricity. Always I remember when it was Remembrance Day, they always had the big service on. There was Jack Kay and his band, and a lot of big bands like that. A lot of comedians, but it wasn't like now, it was quite limited.

Grace Marsden

Morfa Dallimore and Barbara Rose promote a film at the Regal Cinema.

Listening to the Wireless

We had a wireless. I remember my father getting onto me for having it turned up too loud. I would sit down underneath it, listening to Radio Luxemburg or the Ovaltinies. One of the older lads in the street, he was keen on Harry Roy and His Hotshots.

Gordon Mundy

Playing Cards

My father was a very keen card player and used to come into Trowbridge to play cards at the men's club, but if the weather was bad and he couldn't go out, we all had to play cards. We learnt to play whist and bridge.

Vera Taylor

Charlotte Rangers

My brothers and their friends, when they were about seventeen or eighteen, they got up their own football team. It was all friendlies then, the junior football. Along West Ashton road of a Saturday afternoon that was all football. You could go down there and there might be a dozen football matches being played, each side of the road from

Morfa Dallimore dresses up to advertise a film while working as an usherette at the Regal cinema.

Black Ball Hatches. Farmer Corp, we'd go and see him and he'd let you have a field. Mind you had to clear the cow muck. You had to take the goalposts down after your matches and put them up by the sides of the hedges. He never charged us. My brothers' team that they started, was called Charlotte Rangers – Charlotte from our street. I remember their first kit, they had their old cricket shirts and they dyed them and they were supposed to be red. They come out every shade of pink. Some had white shorts, some had black. But you had to get what you could in those days. From being about twelve onwards, I was running the line for them. They all worked Saturday mornings so when I finished my chores, I'd go up and get a sack of sawdust and I used to push that down to West Ashton Road on my bicycle and start marking the pitch. They did come down at 12 o'clock, when they were finished work and help finish off marking. You had to do it by hand, spreading the sawdust. Later on we could afford to do it with a bucket and brush. The Rubber factory, they always had a team, they were in the Trowbridge and District League. There was the Trowbridge Casuals, Trowbridge South, Trowbridge Wanderers. Bowyers had a team down there.

Gordon Mundy

Trowbridge Town

Trowbridge Town they played at the Flower Show Field and then at Bythesea Road, where the County Hall is now. Part of it was allotments, part of it was waste land, trees and shrubs and

The Trowbridge Casuals, *c*. 1950. Gordon Mundy is at the back, far right.

Jack Carter wears the Aston Villa football strip in 1934.

John Almond referees a local game in 1966.

that. It was 1923 when they started playing there, and they moved from there to Frome Road in 1933. We used to sit on the high wall opposite. It was the builder's yard, and we used to get in the yard and climb onto the wall that overlooked the ground and watch the football from there. There were quite a few county players playing then. Alec Batley was the county goal keeper, Harold Nixen, Lewis, Jimmy Ladd and the James brothers.

Jack Carter

Best Field in the West

I used to go now and again to watch Trowbridge play. You had a nice atmosphere, wonderful atmosphere. The original ground was where County Hall's stood on – the best ground in the county. Said that it was the best football field in the west. The people from out the villages used to come out and you used to have four or five thousand there sometimes for a match.

Edgar Davis

Referee

Before the war, my husband used to referee the school football teams in London. When he went into the army he continued to referee and in Trowbridge, even though he only had one eye, they took him on and he got on very well. They used to tell him he couldn't get any higher with refereeing because of his one eye. Otherwise he could have gone on to League football and that. While he was here he always did the local football for the surrounding villages.

Lilian Almond

Gun Carriage Displays

Behind Trinity Church there was the field where they held the Flower Show. That had railings and a gate and that was locked at night. In the evening of the Flower Show, the soldiers from the barracks at Frome Road, they came down with horses pulling a gun carriage and they used to give a display in the field. These horses used to go round crossing over and that. I remember it because just when they got to us one time, one of the horses legs got over the chain. There were four horses, you know two and two, fastened with a chain and one got its leg caught in that. It hurt itself because they couldn't stop for a minute, they were going so fast. I kept saying, 'Is the horse gonna die?' But on our way out the vet was there sewing it up, so Mum said, 'You needn't worry any more, need you!'

Jessie Whitmarsh

Lunch at the George

We used to go to the George for lunch, because that was lovely, the posh place in Trowbridge in those days. I can remember tasting trout for the first time when I went there. They'd covered in the old courtyard – it was an old coaching inn and originally the coaches would go through this sort of square entrance and it would open out into a courtyard. There was a glass roof and you could look up and see how all the rooms were all around this courtyard. They'd glassed it in to make the dining room and that's where we ate. It would have been quite an interesting place to have had still in Trowbridge.

Marion Dutch

New Year's Eve

Outside the Town Hall there used to be a lamp stand in the middle of the road. On New Year's Eve there was always a big ball in the Town Hall, they were all dressed up in nice clothes. At midnight they all used to come out and dance in the street round the lamp. There were crowds of people there and everybody joined in and they sang Old Lang Syne and then the National Anthem. We used to go up there every

A charabanc trip from Trowbridge to Cheddar and Gough's Caves in about 1923. The young man in the large cap to the left is Frank Porter and immediately to his left are: Alice, Evelyn and Mrs Porter.

A winning skittles team from the Central Liberal Club. Harry Smart is seated far right.

New Years Eve. It was great fun.

Jessie Whitmarsh

Playing Skittles

It used to be very safe to walk around. I used to play skittles and I felt quite safe coming out on my own, walking around Trowbridge and that. You'd think nothing of it. We had a skittle alley in the Innox, we also went to Wesley Road, to the Methodist church there and we used to play in their hall at the back. They used to have a silver cup for the winners and a wooden spoon for the losers. We often got the wooden spoon, we never got as far as the cup.

Lilian Almond

A Trip to Weymouth

I don't think I saw the sea till I was seven. My father and stepmother, they decided to go to Weymouth. That was such a thrill, going on the train. When we got near, there was a back water – all dull and grey and I had visions of the sea as a lovely blue sea and I said, 'That isn't the sea is it?' I was disappointed. In those days they had goats pulling little carriages and you'd pay so much, and go along the seafront with this goat pulling you. There was the usual donkeys and I suppose quite a bit of entertainment really. We didn't go much on holidays, that was an exception. It was usually just a day, if anything. The railways did quite a lot of trips in the Summer quite cheaply, excursions like.

Grace Marsden

CHAPTER 6
The war years

The unveiling of the war memorial in Trowbridge Park.

The war memorial, with Palmer and Mackay's mill in the background.

The First Memorial Service

I remember going to the War Memorial, it may have been the first service they had. I know we went from Parochial school and that might have been 1923. They shifted the tank to the side, we used to play in the tank. It was about where the memorial is now, though it wasn't there very long and they moved it from there and put it on a raised dais, kind of thing, with rough stones and that. We used to be able to open the side doors of the tank and get in.

Jack Carter

The Unveiling

I remember the unveiling of the soldier figure in the park. We were let off school and we all went and there was quite a ceremony. They had something draped over it and somebody moved it off. My uncles names are on there. It was quite a thing really.

Grace Marsden

The Tank Taken Away

The park as you know it now, is nothing like it used to be before. The park was a long area and after the First World War, they had a tank given them, as a memorial. In the Second War it was taken away for scrap. They had two avenues of trees going from the old park to the river. Up to that time, the park had just been a long area, almost in the centre of town. When the Second World War came, they opened it up and made a big park and that's why it's like

Traction engines move the tank in Trowbridge Park in 1922 to prepare the area for the war memorial.

it is now. Of course the memorial is right in the centre. I remember being amongst the crowd round that place when it was dedicated.

Fred Hardiman

A Moving Service

I wept when they took the trees down and put some more up. They were all supposed to be in memory of a soldier that died in the First World War. A war widow was supposed to have planted every one. I bet she only put a spade round the top, but every one was planted by a war widow. I remember mum telling me. They were all elms because they live so long and it was a symbol of everlasting life. That was the idea. They always used to have a service down there on Remembrance Day, 11th of November, even if it was in the week in those days, whenever the 11th was. One time I remember it absolutely poured with rain, it just tipped down and Canon Nesbit Wallace at St James' he took the service just the same. He had on his white robes and everything, with poppies pinned at the top and by the time that it was over, he had this red stain all down. It looked like blood. The colour from the poppies had run down his surplice. It was touching. It made it all the worse somehow, to see this blood running down. There was always a good crowd at it. I remember going down to that as a tiny child, we used to go down and my father would say, 'Now stand there and don't you speak.' That was for the two minute silence. In those days there were no railings there, but nobody walked on the grass, we honoured it. I don't remember the Great War, but I was brought up to respect it. During the Second World War, at St James they had a meeting between 1 and 2 o'clock when you could go in and pray. Canon Wallace was always there and we used to pray for peace, every day. And that was the first time that we were ever told, to my knowledge, that we could go without hats. He put a big notice on the gate to say that we were welcome without hats. Quite a few people went and they could go as they were and not have to get all dressed up, like they did on a Sunday. They could come straight out from work.

Jessie Whitmarsh

Sheltering Under the Table

There was one thing in the war I remember, before the air raid shelters were built. The parents whose children lived nearest home, had to have so many children from the other end of town and when the air raid siren sounded, we had to run up to our house at St Thomas' Passage. My Mum used to say, 'Under the table'. There was this great big old fashioned table and we'd have to go under it. Then we'd hear our Mum and the neighbours going, 'Look at that, he's shot him down' and we'd creep out and be stood behind them and then they'd spot us and it would be back under the table. I would've been nine then. Course when they built the shelters in the playgrounds, they were brick built – very, very strong ones. That disappointed us all, because we couldn't see nothing.

Mavis Burt

Evacuees in Trowbridge

In 1938 my husband was in the Regulars and while he was at camp, war broke out and he had to go straight off and never came back from the camp. He was in the Kings Royal Rifles – the KRR. We were right in the middle of the bombing and all that. My eldest son was two years old then and he was affected by the guns and the noise and would wake up in the night. My husband got stationed here in Trowbridge, at the barracks in the Halve, and he found me a place here. So we were evacuees really and from then on we stayed here.

Lilian Almond

A Wartime Wedding

I had lots and lots of things for my bottom drawer. I had a lovely lot of things for my twenty first which all went away. I had a cut glass crystal lemonade set, blankets and sheets. I had a case full of linen that had been my mothers. I saved up lots of little things myself and if I saw anything, I would buy it. We were given lots and lots of things and I used to make a lot of things, you see. But don't forget you always looked for things off coupon and the staff at Knees were very kind. In the china department, the carpet department and the curtain department – if there was anything in there that didn't need a docket, they would leave a message with my aunt. We got all our furniture at Knees. To buy all my bridal clothes, when I got home I used to sit and sew for different people and I kept the money from that to buy my wedding clothes. I also made my sister's dress. I

The announcement of Armistice Day at Trowbridge Town Hall in 1918.

didn't get married in white, because it was a waste of coupons. So I got my outfit from Fear Hills. I took my aunt and Tom's mum with me, so that I got the approval of both. The photos were taken outside Tom's mum's house, because that was where we had the reception. She sat down about forty-six people in the front room and over into the lounge. We all got sat down and all of a sudden the photographer came, so they all had to get up again. We had the *Wiltshire Times* photographer, he had just missed us at the church. We went to North Bradley for our honeymoon, a friend of Tom's was out there. But you just couldn't go anywhere. We went walking, there was no television or anything. We were over there five days altogether.

Enid Hill

A Parcel from America

I can remember when I was at Parochial, everyone got a shoebox or what have you, that the soldiers and the American people had collected, and everyone of us at that school had a gift box. It had a flannel, a little bit of soap, probably little sweets. Things like that in there.

Stanley Jones

Shells for the War

I was born in Dursley Road in 1913. I had two brothers and my father worked in Hadens, which was an engineering firm in Trowbridge, and the war was coming on and he was very occupied with making shells. He was a foreman and he had to go to work such a lot, putting the night shift on and all, because they were making shells for the First World War.

Grace Marsden

The Ammunition Works

There was a factory behind Pitts, it was for metal manufacture. They did some making of shells there, not live shells, but the casings for shells in the iron works behind there. During the Great War that was developed quite a lot.

Fred Hardiman

A leaflet for War Weapons Week dropped from an aeroplane in 1940.

Spitfire Parts

During the war there were several places around Trowbridge making the parts for the Spitfires. The people from Southampton, from the works that had been bombed, came to work at Trowbridge and Southwick. They had places down on Bradley Road, also where the KwikSave used to be, and up Victoria Road. We used to work from 8 o'clock in a morning until 8 o'clock at night. We done a bit of everything. When we went to Southwick first, we were making wings for the Spitfires. We had the ribs and we made the whole wing.

Joyce Hunt

Swarms of People

The Spitfire factory on Bradley Road, they built that during the war, because of the continuous bombing of Southampton where the original factory was. Vickers dispersed the production all over the place. There was Barnes' at Southwick, there was a place down Castle Street, loads of places to avoid the bombs. Bradley Road used to come to a full stop after they built the Spitfire factory. Hundreds of people on bicycles, swarms of them, coming out at the end of shifts.

Max Connor

Air Raid Post

At the clinic we were the air raid post of the town. We had all the St John's

Staff of Haden's Engineering works during the 1914-18 war, during which time the firm was involved in making ammunitions.

ambulance. It was manned every night, fire watching, you name it we had it there. We used to be up all hours making coffee and biscuits. We used to have the warnings over the telephone. My Mum asked me to go out one night, there was all these flares gone up and she'd never seen them before that.

Joyce Hunt

Trowbridge Bombed

When the bombs dropped on Trowbridge, my dad was down at Clarks with uncle Bert and it was the one morning they left early. They weren't supposed to. There used to be a row of cottages behind Clarks and Uncle Bert lived there and dad had just got in the door when the bombs dropped and course they had to turn round and go straight back. The very room that dad and him would have been in, had been hit. Mum came into my room and I was sound asleep, but part of the ceiling had come down. I think it was two were killed down Stallard Street, where the pub used to be.

Mavis Burt

A Good Life for the Officers

The war came when I was about sixteen and I was in the WVS, working over at Holt. We used to have a canteen in what was the village hall. We cooked the meals there and we used to take them out to the schools. When Bath was bombed we had to take the meals down there. Father had a car, a family car and we would go down to Lyme Regis. During the war there was very little petrol. My father had some allowance, because he had to go up to Stroud, Nailsworth and Stroud, to mills up there on business. He had to make a list of everything he was doing. Sometimes we would go with him, as an outing, because you couldn't go anywhere else, except by train. Eventually there was no ration and the old car was laid up on bricks in the garage. The Army took over part of the mill. It was empty at the time and the soldiers were billeted in there. All day long there were Army lorries going up and down. My father used to tell the soldiers off, because the girls would be working in the other part and the soldiers would talk to them and try to get off with them. They used to go off for route marches from there. The Green Howards, they were there. We had two officers billeted with us. They slept in the room at the back and they had two batmen. They slept in the other part that was our nursery. Jock and Taffy they were called. They looked

A demonstration for extinguishing incendiary bombs given in the Market Yard in January 1941. The event was attended by hundreds of Trowbridgians, old and young.

Garnet Dallimore was captured during the retreat to Dunkirk and spent the remainder of the war in prison camps in Poland and Germany.

after the two officers, who had quite a good life as far as I could see. Waited on hand and foot. They used to come and have a drink with us sometimes. Latterly we had the Americans came. We had two medical officers then, one was a dentist and the other was in psychiatry. They both came from New York. They had a dance once, for all the people they'd been billeted with, I remember going to that.

Anne Mackay

Helping the War Effort

We used to have a playing field up the top of Whaddon Lane, with swings and that. When the war came the whole field was covered with flax. We used to go picking up potatoes and that on the local farms. We got a few pence an hour for doing it, but it was pocket money and we thought it was wonderful. We'd walk into Trowbridge and go to the cinema. Buses were few and far between and with my mother being a widow with five of us, money was hard to come by. During the war my mother looked after another woman's three children. She used to clean a doctors house and two other houses. The other woman had been called into the factory and if you had young children of your own you had to help out. We had an evacuee couple living in our sitting room. They worked at the dairy, Nestle's, he was an engineer. All the family had come and the children and that were billeted around the street. They were called key workers. If you didn't take in evacuees, you took in some of the workers. If you had a spare room, they took it. They had to eat and sleep and everything in the one room and it wasn't very big. We collected jam jars, books and papers, rags and bones. The books we took to Nelson Haden school for the war effort. Jam jars and lemonade bottles and that had to go back to the shops. Everything that came in a bottle, even the bleach bottles had to go back. If you had medicine you had to pay a shilling for the bottle and you got your money back when you returned the bottle. We got our medicine from Boots or Aplins or the Co-op, they had a chemist there later years. One of the playing fields at Nelson Haden, what used to be the boys playing field, was taken over by the Army. They used it as their playing fields. It was fenced off. The

soldiers used to do manoeuvres and when you were coming back from town, you'd see these barricades across the road and see these soldiers laying down. I suppose it was practise before they were sent abroad. Many a times you'd come across them. There was the Spitfire factory on the Hilperton Road, they made the ball bearings for the Spitfires there. One time we were coming along the top road and there was somebody taking photographs and they were picked up by the police.

Dorothy Walton

Shopping with Coupons

I used to come home from work with about three pounds – and my mum had two and I had one. I spent it on sweets – I was a chocolate fanatic. I used to buy sweet coupons off people. You could get

Jack and Joyce Carter photographed at Houlton's photographers in 1942, when Jack was on leave.

quarter of a pound a week of sweets on ration and that was if they had them. I shall never forget one day in the war. Mum had gone down town to get some oranges one of the shops had in and when she got home she realised they hadn't marked my brothers book, so she sent me back down and we got a double lot of oranges. At Christmas you used to barter. If somebody had something what you wanted, you'd barter and swap to get it. We kept chickens and Mum would swap one to get what she wanted. I remember Mum wanted some wall paper one year, and she knew someone who had some and she said, 'Well, I'll give you a chicken if you let me have that wall paper'.

Mavis Burt

Volunteers for the RAF

Course the war came on and they could keep apprentices back, but as time went on there wasn't so much work for us to do at the *Wiltshire Times*. We'd find ourselves doing the menial jobs, we were getting a bit fed up and being young and stupid, we thought we'd go and volunteer. That was the kind of thing then, but the craze was to get into the RAF as wireless operation air gunners. We went down to Bristol, myself and two of my mates. I was the only one who got through. When your papers come through I had to go and tell Mr Lansdown and he didn't like it and he said, 'Well you've made your bed, you'll have to lie in it', kind of thing.

Gordon Mundy

Taking the Railings

We used to get up when the air raids went and look out of the back window. We had our picture taken at McCalls all standing in the tank, what was for an air raid shelter. We got so we took no notice, you'd hear the hooters, you know air raid and that, and the silence, and then you'd go back to work. We never had it quite so bad here, it was mostly Bristol and Bath. There was a bomb at Town Bridge, and one just down Dursley Road. They took all the railings for the war work. Round Rodney House there was all these railings, and they went all the way down to Trowbridge Park.

Alice Smart

An Army Town

The army had spread out in Trowbridge during the war, and they took over the whole of St Thomas's Road, we called it Middle Lane then, and from the Halve right through to Rodwell Park every part of it was taken by the army. All the houses – Bellefield House, Hilbury Court, Rodwell Park were all officers quarters All the soldiers were camped in the grounds. All the young soldiers were being trained there and then it all went quiet for a little while and then we had the Americans there before D-Day. Union Street was just a huge tank park, both sides of the road, right the way as far as Zion Chapel. One of the bungalows in St Thomas Road, if you look carefully, has a high stone wall and you can see a curve where it was repaired. In the

Dorothy Walton's mother, Lucy, dressed in her brother's uniform during the First World War.

middle of the war, that wall was completely demolished. The black Americans had lovely singing voices, and if you went up St Thomas Road of an evening , they'd be sitting in that gap where those bungalows are, singing just like church choirs. It was wonderful really. Being children like, we used to run behind the Americans and the favourite call then was, 'Any gum chum?'

Stanley Jones

RHA on Parade

During the war years, Wesley Road used to get packed with American soldiers and they used to parade to our church from the barracks or wherever they were. The Royal Horse Artillery, they used to go on parade to Holy Trinity church. On one occasion we went down to watch them out and the bugler, he was missing and he was running all up Newtown to try and catch up and be with them. What had happened was, he came out the little back door and the others came out of the front. It was laughable, but I bet he got into awful trouble.

Enid Hill

Soldier's Wash Days

During the war the Bethesda church hall was used for a class of evacuee children, pending their transfer to other schools. Every home, where possible, had one or more of these children. Many attended our Sunday School. The hall was also used to billet about one hundred soldiers. We had a room near the gate that was used as a small rest room. A number of them attended worship during their short stay in the hall. The soldiers drained the boiler for hot water on their 'wash days' Towards the end of the war the hall was divided into office cubicles and used by the Ministry of Labour.

Fred Hardiman

Blown Out of Bed

The stick of bombs fell at about half past six, I think we were getting a little bit complacent with the raids in those days, we were in bed at any rate – whether the sirens had gone or not. From where we lived in Union Street down to Town Bridge as the crow flies is not far. It was the biggest bang I have ever heard, the whole house shook and I remember my Mum dashing to the window and she said, 'Bert, that one was close, wasn't it' and I always joked I was never sure whether we were blown out of bed or jumped out. Any rate we didn't stay in bed any longer. My Dad was working for Ushers then, and he used to go early because he was on the transport. He came back about half an hour later and I remember him looking up at the bedroom window at my Mum. He was very dramatic. He said, Town Bridge has been bombed. There's no windows left up the Parade, all the windows are out up to the station.' This stick of bombs had hit the Mill House and we went down in the evening and

had a look and it was completely over the road. It took a direct hit and two people were killed there and where the road is widened on the other side of the river, there was an old public house there and that was bombed and that was a single storey building for years after. The other bomb landed yards from the main gasometer. There was a full gasworks then and the bomb landed right in the gasworks gate and all the buildings behind what was Sharp and Fisher were demolished and the windows were all blown out, virtually as far as Lloyds Bank and the other way virtually up to Bythesea Road. Those windows weren't replaced until the end of the war. In those days they sort of boarded the windows up and left like about two foot square, so that people could get a little bit of light in. All the windows up Wicker Hill, all through the war, were just with little glass peep holes.

During the war years the car park for the market was used by the army as a lorry park, except for market days and they would all clear out then and the army lorries used to park along Brown Street. The market hall was used as a government food depot in the war, for meat and things like that, so there wasn't any indoor market during the war and the stalls would be on the approach road to the cattle market as you went down.

Stanley Jones

Visited by the Queen

In 1943 the old Queen Mary came and looked around the mill. She lived at

Queen Mary with Major Mackay at Hilperton, following her visit to the Trowbridge mills in 1943.

Badminton during the war. She was very stately. My mother and I had to assemble up in the office block, my mother in her Red Cross uniform and I had my WVS outfit on. I had this bouquet, I was supposed to curtsey and then say, 'Will you accept this bouquet Ma'am?' Instead of that I said, 'How do you do' and shook her hand and she said, 'How do you do?' or, 'How are you?' Something like that. She was very informal, not at all aloof in her manner. I had to shake hands with the Princess Royal as well. I was so frightened, but she was very kind. She went up to tea at Hilperton, to my uncle Eric Mackay. She would admire everything and you felt that you had to offer her something. She was well known for doing that and he gave her some china, I believe. He collected china and would have had some nice things.

Anne Mackay

CHAPTER 7
Trowbridge life

The Royal Guard of Honour, L Neery Battery, in the late 1930s. Bombadier George Hunt is standing on the far left.

View of the Conigre chapel and nearby buildings in 1958.

The Royal Horse Artillery

The RHA, Royal Horse Artillery, were stationed at Trowbridge and every morning the horses were taken for exercise. Around half past seven, they would come out of the barracks in Bradley Road, come all down through the town, up Conigre hill, along Upper Broad Street and then back into the town again, giving the horses exercise up these hills. Every morning we could almost wake up and see all the trail of horses. In those days Trowbridge was called a military town, where the RHA was based. I remember as a boy we used to play football against them.

Fred Hardiman

The Badges

I was courting at thirteen and I got married at just seventeen. My husband was at the barracks in the Royal Horse Artillery – L Neery Battery. He was from Bexleyheath in London. He had joined up at fourteen in Woolwich and won his silver bugle. He was a trumpeter and they were always called Badges. I think they were the first out to France in the war, because they had the Howitzer guns. A lot of the RHA married Trowbridge girls.

Joyce Hunt

A Ha'pennyworth of Chips

In Shails Lane there was a lodging house and it was managed by Cliff who lived in Upper Broad Street. It was just a big open barn-type place. You approached it going down three or four steps. As children, we would go round and peep through the door and run. This was where the vagrants and the homeless ended up. There was a stove where they could cook on. Spaces were marked out like car parking spaces and it was just bare floor, no beds, and they laid their own bedding down and that was it. Milton was the rag and bone man, you could always sell a rabbit skin there for thre'pence or fourpence. His wife had a fish and chip cart – Mary Milton, with a fire in it, and she cooked her chips on it. They always had their skins on. You could get a halfpenny worth of chips and she would drive round with this cart from about 7 o'clock at night. The cart had a sunken floor so that children could reach the counter.

John Reynolds

Cheating at the Soup Kitchen

I went in the soup kitchen with my big jug. The thing was my mother was a bit of a character you see. We had one ticket and she did always make out her own ticket for the soup. She had one ticket and she would get the colour of the card and make her own ticket out of something! I didn't like that idea. I didn't mind going down with the real one, but we had to go. We did as we were told then. And it was good, I always enjoyed it. All the kiddies who were home for their dinner hour, they were all sent by their mothers and fathers most of the time. You had to get in the queue and they did dish it out into these big

jugs. I can always remember my mother doing this trick, but I never remember it ever being queried.

Gordon Mundy

Weavers' Cottages

We lived in Dymott Square in Hilperton and we had gas lights and a gas stove and we had to fetch all the water from the tap outside in a bucket and take it in. It was one tap between six houses and the next set of houses down through the arch, they had to share. They'd put in some new toilets, down the path, so we had our own in the Square.

If you went in the front door, you were in the passageway and there was a door on each side and the stairs went straight up. The kitchen was very large, with a larder behind. They were weavers' cottages and course there was big windows out the back, for the light for the looms. That's what made the other rooms so small. In the big bedroom you could get two double beds and a single bed in. You had two big windows and one little small one at the back. The sitting room had two big windows as well. In the kitchen there was just the one little window and one at the back. The larder was the big room where they used the looms, that had two huge windows there. Under the stairs we used as the coal house, because it was rationed and if you didn't look after it, it would disappear. We got our coal from Bird's on Station Approach and he brought it on his horse and cart.

Dorothy Walton

Little More than a Hovel

Our house in Mortimer Street, well the door opened in to a room, and that was your front room, then another door led into your kitchen, where you ate. You only had the two rooms and the same upstairs. You had no bathroom, no toilets, you had to go outside for your toilet and you had communal toilets out there you see. You shared a communal tap outside as well, so if you had a bath you had to have a tin bath in front of the fire. Of course if you had a nice fire you'd have toast, you'd have your toasting fork, used to do the bloaters, fresh herrings. 'Twas a very plain house, I suppose the modern generation might call it a hovel really, just the two rooms down and the two rooms up. We lived at number 4 Mortimer Street and in the floods we had to go upstairs, so we used to get the food out of the pantry and take it upstairs with us. Course you didn't know whether you were up there one day – two days. On this one particular occasion when it was really deep, we were caught unawares and had no food nor nothing then. We were upstairs for a couple of days and as it subsided, there was a neighbour who was a fireman working for Ushers, he went out with two chairs with his boots on and that, and sort of walked his way through the water up to the corner shop and got some bread and we opened the bedroom windows and he just threw the bread through the windows and we had dry bread, but at least it was something

View of St Thomas's Passage, now demolished, showing nos 7–14. Mavis Burt (nee Neal) lived at no. 11, the house with the greenhouse.

102

to eat. When the floods were up they used to have the horse and carts and they used to sit on the carts and pay a penny to go across. If they couldn't get through in Mortimer Street, then they couldn't get through from Town Bridge, because the Town Bridge floods used to come up first, and the waters come up higher than in Mortimer Street. They were cut off from their work, so of course they'd pay their penny and the horse and cart dealers use to do a trade, taking them backwards and forwards to work.

Jack Carter

Doing the Washing

We lived in St Thomas's Passage, number eleven. You had your tap outside, your toilet outside, and the boiler was in what you called the scullery in them days. You had to light a fire underneath it to get hot water. And the coal house was there in the scullery. We had a lovely front garden. We had a real smart front room. The door went in to a passage and at the side was the kitchen living room where we used to eat and then through the passage there was another door and that took you to a room looking out into the back garden and that was like your best room. Mum always done the washing while we were at school and that was hard work. I used to help with the ironing, you know, and that was with the old-fashioned irons that you put on the fire or on the gas ring to heat them up. You couldn't control them like you can today.

Mavis Burt

Named After Lloyd George

My mother's mother, she was marvellous. She lived in New Road in Trowbridge and her door was always open for us. We could always go there any time and she always had a piece of cake for us. She had an old-fashioned grate that you cooked in the side of and she always had her fire going all the time. When she did vegetables, she'd put them on the back of the fire, sometimes she'd put some water on to make it last or something and all the dust would spray out. In those days there was a lot of dust. Her husband died in 1916, the same year as my mother died and he was a painter and decorator for Gould and Stephens, they used to be a firm in Trowbridge. When he died there was no pension and she used to take in laundering these stiff collars for the business people. It was ever such a skilled job. She had this rounded iron and they had to be done carefully, you hadn't to get any dust on those, mind. She thought Lloyd George was wonderful, because he brought in the pension. Ten shillings a week. I know a lot of people who called their son Lloyd George in memory of him, because they thought it was such a wonderful thing to have a pension. She wouldn't have had one see and they dreaded going to the workhouse, that was at Semington. That was an awful thing to go to the workhouse, that was the lowest thing of any. Later they made it a hospital for old people, but for them it was always the workhouse, and she had to go there and she thought it was awful ending up there even though it was no longer the workhouse.

Grace Marsden

103

Trowbridge and District Hospital

I can remember when I was very young, my mother and father were caretakers at the clinic, which was then along Bythesea Road. We then moved to the Trowbridge and District Hospital at the Halve. The hospital was a big place, all the wards were different clinics like orthopaedics and dentists. Everything was done there at that time. For children, baby clinics, you name it, it was there. We had a lot of the big specialists from Bath, the RUH, come up and each day there was something different done there.

Joyce Hunt

Avoiding the Doctor

I didn't have any contact with the doctor or the hospital until I was fourteen, you tried to avoid it if you could. When my brother joined the Post Office he had to have a medical and see a dentist. He tells the tale of the dentist when he went there to extract a tooth. It was half a crown, but they would do it for sixpence if you didn't have the cocaine. He had it without cocaine, so he said.

John Reynolds

The Fever Ambulance

One of the grocers in Silver Street was also an ambulance man, Mr

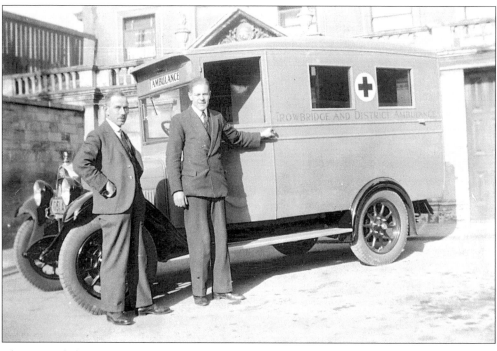

The new ambulance provided by the Committee of the Trowbridge and District Hospital Carnival in 1939.

ME OF MEMBER *James R Avon* .... RATE OF CONTRIBUTION *3½wkl*

DRESS *2 Dymont Rd. Hilperton* .... FIRM OR GROUP *Hilperton*

MES OF DEPENDENTS .... DATE OF BIRTH* ....

Eilen L. A. Avon .... „ 4 /2 /1929

Dorothy V. .... „ 1 /12 /1930

William A. J. „ .... „ 30 /3 /1932

Robert F. „ .... „ 28 /1 /1934

Roger C „ .... 10 /12 /1935

On admission to the Hospital a member must produce a Certificate of Membership
he Scheme, signed by the Group Secretary, or other responsible person.
*This is required for young persons and children only.

1 /2 /32

Trowbridge and District Hospital Contributory Scheme, objects and rules. This record card for the Avons family dates from 1929.

Before the NHS

We paid into a scheme, there was the Pioneer and the West Wilts Conservatives and they had these schemes and you paid so much a week. One lot was at Bridge House and the other was down on the corner of Hill Street and Wicker Hill. There were other ones. I think my Dad was in the Oddfellows. There was lots of these different schemes to help pay for health and that. Some people were on the committee and then when it came to, you had help with paying for the doctor and that. I think a bottle of medicine was 3/6, which was a lot then, when you didn't have much money. If you went in the hospital, it was ever such poor food and your family were expected to bring you in eggs and nourishing food. The hospital was in the Halve where the

Boulter. There were two ambulances in Trowbridge in those days. The ordinary ambulance that took you to Trowbridge hospital and the fever ambulance. Now the fever ambulance was a little brown old van and that used to strike horror into people, because that took you up to the fever hospital up at St Johns. If an ambulance was needed, Mr Boulter would leave his shop and go and get the ambulance from wherever it was kept. During the war there was also an emergency ambulance, I think it was provided by Ushers. During the day the local fire engine was stood at the top of Timbrell Street, there by the County Ground. It would do the rounds and an Ushers van was the ambulance and would follow it around during air raids just in case it was needed.

Stanley Jones

clinic is now.

Grace Marsden

Fish Tail Lights

We had what you call incandescent lights, that you could pull a kind of thing to light it. In the other room we had two upright gas ones and the mantles would break if you weren't careful. When you bought the mantle it was done up with something to keep it firm and you had to burn that off and then it was ever so fragile and you had to be careful when you lit it not to break it. Then you had the glass on top. Upstairs you had something called fishtails. They were in the shape of fish tails and they were open. Ever so dangerous, when I think of it, this open flame with nothing over them at all. It gave off a bit of heat sometimes as well, if you were poorly.

Grace Marsden

Pumping up Water

We didn't have electricity until I was fifteen. We had oil lamps. We had paraffin oil, we used to get it from Knees, in a tin can. They were free standing lamps and then you had a candle to take upstairs. We didn't have a bathroom until the electricity came,

The Earl family, *c.* 1910. The family were well known locally as brushmakers and repairers. Left to right, back row: Alf, Walter, Sam, Bill, Fred. Middle: Laura, Alfred and Kate (née Harris). Front: Arthur and Ernest.

then we had one of the bedrooms divided up to make the bathroom. Before that it was a tin bath in the kitchen. We had a toilet upstairs, that was one of our jobs, we took it in turns to pump the water. The pump was in the scullery. You had to pump the handle and it sent the water upstairs to a tank for the toilet. It had to be done about once a day to fill the tank. So every day we would have to take it in turns to pump the water up. In our bedrooms we had a wash stand with a marble top and you had your basin stood on that.

Vera Taylor

No Toilet Paper

These houses in Ashton Street, they were workmen's houses really, workers for the clothmills, I suppose. They never had bathrooms. Toilets were always outside, we had no water closet like, you had a bucket of water out there and the one that used it had to fill the bucket and there was always an outcry when they hadn't done it. No toilet paper, we had to cut newspapers up and put them on a string.

Grace Marsden

A Bedside Table

All the houses that I knew of in the Conigre area, they had gas downstairs and used a candle upstairs. I made a table to go at our bedside for the candle to stand on. It was an old box and I nailed a leg at each corner and then turned it upside down. The bottom of the box was the top of the table. Mother put a piece of material on there and it looked alright in the bedroom, by the side of the bed. That was the first bedside table I had!

Fred Hardiman

Life at Courtfield House

First of all the mill was Palmer and Brown and my two great uncles came down from Scotland and got into the business. Later it became Palmer and Mackay. It seemed to do very well. I got to know some of the people, they'd worked there all their lives some of them. They lived locally in Ashton Street, Polebarn Road, all those cottages were built for weavers for the mill. I can remember seeing the people walking past the house when I was small. We had a big garden and the orchard and someone used to come and cut the hay with one of those big scythes. He'd cut the grass and pile it onto a little pony cart and take it away. We'd spend hours down there as children, mucking about, playing. It always seemed to be warm summers in those days. We also used to have geese down in the orchard, I suppose they helped to keep the grass down, but they were nasty, snappy things.

We had a cook living in and when I was a small child, we had a parlour maid. She used to wait on table to us. In those days they were paid quite well and they lived in the two rooms at the top of the house. They used to come and go, they didn't stay very long. They got good food, good meals. Whatever we

A Trowbridge Urban District Council election leaflet from 1923.

had they had as well. Later on, we used to have people in to clean the house, but during the war it became difficult to get anyone and we had to set to and do it ourselves. Thankfully Mother enjoyed cooking.

Anne Mackay

Keeping House

I didn't ever really work, but I used to keep house while my mum and dad ran the shop. We had a big house, we had fourteen rooms. I used to do the washing with mum, that was in the shed at the back. We had a copper with a fire underneath – you heated the water in there. You had to fill that with a bucket from the tap. Mum used to boil her puddings and all in there, tied in a piece of cloth. You'd boil them pretty well all day and you would be back and forth making the fire up. She used to make about seven – one for everybody's birthday. They kept well in those days.

My mother had a board what you rub your clothes up on and a piece of soap, Sunlight, I think it was, in a bar. Then we had the wringer, an iron one with wooden rollers and you had two galvanised baths with your cold water for rinsing. I remember one time it was frozen and mum brought in snow and melted that. We had a yard that you could hang the washing out in. We had an inside toilet and we had a bath, but you had to carry your hot water from the copper up for it. Carry it indoors from the back yard, through the passage, up the stairs and along another passage to the bathroom. We all used to have a bath the same day, everybody adding to it. You could let the water out from the bath, you didn't have to carry it down again. We didn't have any hot water in the kitchen. You had to put a kettle on the gas stove to get hot water. We just had a sink to do the washing up in and a table by the side of it, what we used to put a tray on for draining. We never had a drainer. The sink was dark, a kind of reddish, but we always bought a washing up bowl and put that in it and used it. The sink was shallow. We had a gas stove. We had a fire with bars across it, that we had to

108

black lead. It had two little things on the side where you could boil a kettle or cook a stew, mum would put it on the side there and it would go on all day. We didn't have electric irons, they were gas irons and you used to heat them on the side of the fire. You took the kettle of hot water upstairs to wash, you had a big china bowl in your bedroom. You kept the jug filled with cold water up there and you had a pail for emptying the bowls and to carry it downstairs.

Jessie Whitmarsh

The King and Queen Visited

You didn't have cars, there was no cars about, it was all horse and carts. There were very few cars. I remember Queen Mary and King George came here in 1917 and they had a car, we were so interested in seeing the car more than them! I was so disappointed, because I thought they would be Kings and Queens in their robes, but he was just an oldish man to me, in a bowler hat and her in her toque hat and that. We were by the Town Hall. Over the road from there, there was a grocer's shop and they put loads and loads of tea boxes out, so that you could stand on them. People lifted you on to these if you were smaller, like the children. It was quite something to see a car.

Grace Marsden

The Salvation Army Band

The Salvation Army, they used to play outside the George Hotel every Saturday evening. They were very good and they had a lovely band in those days. They used to play and read *The*

An early photograph of the Trowbridge fire brigade.

Bible and say a few words. Lots of people used to stop and listen. Saturday was a busy day and the shops were open to nine o clock. So there were a lot of people about. Where the Salvation Army Citadel is, that was where they used to keep the fire engine. When there was a fire, the siren went and we used to rush round to see the fire engine go out. There were no permanent firemen, they all rushed out of work and came on their bicycles in those days. I think I can even remember when it was drawn by horses. The hooters went off at set times, morning and evening and if it went off in between, we knew it was a fire or something.

Jessie Whitmarsh

Always Something to See

A very interesting street was Court Street, as there was the cloth mills and the cloth being taken from one part of the factory to another. There was a place where you used to be able to go in and buy oddments. There was always something to see along there. At Chapmans we could watch the bed frames and that being made and we saw the straw being delivered for the beds or palliasses. At Pikes, the wheelwright, we could watch spokes and wheels being made for the traps and small carts. Then there was the GWR stables. We could watch the horses being groomed. And there was Avons brush factory. You could look through the windows and watch the girls putting bristles, etc, into the heads of brooms. Wiggins the blacksmiths, was next and you could watch the rims being put on cart wheels

and the horse shoes being made and the horses being shod. Clevelands – that was a butcher and slaughterman and we would watch the cows and calves being skinned and cut up. At the Co-op bakery we'd watch the vans being loaded and the bread, etc, coming out of the ovens. It was fascinating when we were lads, always something to see.

Jack Carter

Drinking Fountains

There were three drinking fountains – one in Bythesea Road and two in Fore Street, one by Garlickes shop and the other one was round by Elloways, which was down where the Portman Building Society is now. Three water fountains, they were for animals, with a trough round them, but we used to drink from them. The water was fresh. We used to drink out of the spout.

Jack Carter

A Cow in the Shop

The cattle market, now the entrance to that was through a little road that went down beside some ladies toilets at the back of Sylvester and Macketts. As you went down, on the left and on the right were all the cattle pens and the selling would be going on in the middle of the market. In those days there was a lot of shouting and the auctioneers selling and on the back by Castle Street there was rows of poultry, chickens and that. Tuesdays, market day was really busy. You used to see the cattle, sometimes they would be going to the market and sometimes they'd be going to the abattoirs. You were always getting shop windows smashed with cows going into them. My sister worked in Aplins as an assistant for years, I can remember her coming home and saying, 'We've had a cow in the shop today'. The public houses, they closed at two o' clock, but market day, the pubs were allowed to stay open till half past three or four. By then the local pubs would be full of the farmers all having their drinks and down in the market they'd be all clearing up.

Stanley Jones

Keeping an Allotment

I think people tried to keep their front gardens nice, their houses painted up and their gardens nice. They all had allotments, they all tried to grow food for most of the year and there were allotments at the top of this road, Ashton Street. It was always quite an entertainment – all the men would go up there and they'd say, 'old so-and-so has got his potatoes up', and that sort of thing, and it was quite an entertainment really. We all got involved, you know, when the potatoes had to be dug up, the boys had to help. Most things were grown out of your garden. It was healthier really when you think of it. There were very few easy foods. Everything was well cooked.

Grace Marsden

A procession through Fore Street on the occasion of the death of Edward VII in 1910.

Trowbridge Characters

The one big character that everyone still talks about from the old days is old Joe Collins. He was a funny old man, a handy man, window cleaner, bicycle cleaner. He lived on the corner of Charlotte Street and if you ever looked in his door, it was nothing but old coats and rags in there. He used to wear about three or four overcoats, a bowler hat and always had an umbrella over his shoulder. He had an old bicycle and he would go down through the town. He was handyman for everything. When I was at County Hall, he would see a bicycle there and clean it and than wait for someone to come along for the

111

money. Then there was old Mr Marsh. He was the one come round with the vegetables on a horse and cart. There were quite a few old tramps about in those days – there was one called Henry, he used to sit on the steps of Lloyd's Bank. In those days there were people still suffering from the First World War, and you'd see men going around with one leg – there were no artificial limbs, it was a common sight. I didn't realise it then, but they were probably soldiers from the Great War.

Stanley Jones

Collecting the Rent

We used to collect all the council rents. The council only had two fellows collecting and they used to visit every house, every week collecting the money. Life was different and people used to be so honest, they used to leave the front door unlocked, leave the rent on the mantelpiece and our chap used to go in and get it. We had one housing manager and two rent collectors and about nineteen hundred council houses. It was a lot of houses, but they'd collect all the money and the clerk was responsible for the whole thing balancing up.

Noel Knee

A production of the *Flag Lieutenant* by the Trowbridge Amateur Dramatic Society in the Town Hall. Charlie Taylor is standing at the back, centre. He was a well known local shopkeeper and a singer in the society and in St James' choir.

New Fangled Stuff – Electricity

Mr Powell, he lived at Park Street, he turned the gas lamps on. He cycled round and he had a long pole and he'd come along in the evening, put it on like at dusk and then come round next morning and turn it out. We used to play round these posts at night, when the lights came on, because it was quite safe or it seemed to be safe in those days. I remember when electricity came to Trowbridge. They started up what they called WestCo. and they wanted to try out street lights and they tried Ashton Street. There was three lights, but they had a clock to come on and off and they would always go wrong. Sometimes the lights were on all day and not on at night and so on and all the people voted against that. In no way did they want that, but eventually it came. When the electricity really started, they would put three lights in and one plug free. My Dad wouldn't have that – not new fangled stuff. He didn't want none of that and he didn't have it for several years.

Grace Marsden

A Healthy Respect for a Copper

You had a healthy respect for the police in those days. You had to. We respected them, you know, we'd run a mile if we saw a policeman, there's no doubt about it. Whether we had been doing something wrong or not. But we used to get up to mischief. Knock on people's doors, tie a bit of string along from one door to another and that.

Jack Carter

No Parking

My father had a bicycle and I used to ride behind him when I was very little and I used to fall asleep, leaning to the side. Then he got a car, a Morris Bull Nose. He used to park it up Bradford Road. Living in Church Walk, he couldn't park it there. Later he parked it in Conigre. Up the top there was a big house what had two or three garages, Needhams, and he parked it there for a time. When people started to buy cars, nobody had garages, and you had to come to a private arrangement to find somewhere to park it.

Jessie Whitmarsh

The Cheesemaker

In the Summer, the lorry used to come from Nestle's factory to collect the milk in churns. Someone from Walden's used to send a man round the farms collecting eggs. We had a dairy and a cheesemaker lived there and in the Winter she made cheese. She made Cheddar cheese. She was a very good cheesemaker, because my father used to show the cheese in Frome Show and they used to win prizes for it. It wasn't very common to have a cheesemaker, there weren't many farms at that time making cheese. I didn't have to help with the cheese, but sometimes we would go and watch her making it. They had a huge tub they put the milk in, really large, and then she would add rennet overnight and then you'd get the curds form. She would chop that up. Then it had to be put into a container and into a press, which they tightened up and that would form the

An outing for the staff of the Modeluxe Laundry in 1957.

cheese. They were quite large and they used to store the cheese in one of the rooms of the old house. Someone used to come from Wells to collect the cheese.

Vera Taylor

Living with Rats

I can remember once this man were coming down in his car, about 12 o'clock at night, and when they demolished McCall's mill, he said it was swarming and swarming with rats. He could see them with his car lights. So he stopped and they were all rushing across the road. It was down at St Stephens Place, down there. There used to be some houses belonged to the factory there and course they got rid of all them

as well. He said he'd never seen nothing like it. He made a report about them and they said they must have come from when they pulled the factory down. Course, we had rats at the factory where I worked and we used to stop the dinner some times. We used to sit in the slay room [????], where they used to keep all the slays. It was nothing to see one dart under one of the slays and we'd tell the foreman and he'd go down and underneath was a cellar and he'd go down and put some poison. I don't know whether it got rid of any or not.

Lilly Pickett

CHAPTER 8

Church life

A gathering outside the old Bethesda chapel in Court Street, taken in the 1920s. Pastor Olney Davies and his wife are seated in the centre of the picture.

Manvers Street Methodist church was built in 1836 and demolished in 1972. Its congregation joined that of the Tabernacle in 1968.

Sunday School Treats

Whit Tuesday was a big day when we walked round the town with all the other Sunday schools. We all had our banners and each school went to a different field for games and races. If it was wet, we used to hire the Market Hall. At the end of the treat each child was given a bag with a piece of cake in it.

Winnie Caines

Aerial Railway

I remember the aerial railway that Mr White used to put up. You went in a basket down this aerial railway, which was hung between two trees. When we got older we had to catch hold of the handles and go bump on to a sack of hay at the bottom. I will say, I can remember the Centenary Anniversary in 1928. The only time I can remember anything like it in our chapel. All the seats were packed and we had to put seats right down the aisles. We were upstairs with the children. I don't think it was quite packed at the top, but we had seats in the aisles.

Kathleen Hooper

Sunday School Teacher

We had a dear teacher, Annie Gore, and I used to sit right in front of her and she would teach us all the little children's things – What a friend we have in Jesus, There's a friend for little children, things like that. She was a lovely Christian lady. She would tell us the stories about Jesus in a very simple way, but enough to know about the real Gospel message of Jesus dying for us.

Mary Martin

A Huge Part of Our Lives

We had some fun in our church life, in our Bible classes and that. Our teacher was a Mrs Boulter, that had a fruit shop in Silver Street. Her husband was the Superintendent of the Sunday school. We also had a Mr James, who was James Brothers down on the Parade with electrical equipment. He took us on the morning, Mr Boulter was in the afternoon and a Mr Harding, Freddie Harding who lived along Wyke Road, he was the Deputy and would come along if someone wasn't there to officiate. Mrs Boulter used to get concert evenings off the ground, like if it was a Guild evening. Get the Bible class girls to perform. I was in the choir at Wesley Road and I also was missionary secretary, collecting monies every Sunday. I used to go to Methodist Guild on Tuesday nights and choir practise Thursday nights. So it was a huge part of our lives. We had several ministers over the years – Mr Viney, who married us, Mr Dyer was superintendent minister, Revd Elliot and Revd Tennant.

Enid Hill

Picture of the Caines family who were members of the Zion chapel. Miss Winnie Caines, centre, taught Sunday school for many years.

The Avons family who sang in the choir at St Michael and All Angels Church, Hilperton. From left to right: Bill, Dorothy, Mrs Avons, Eileen and Bob. In front, Roger. The picture was taken in the early 1940s.

Church Choir Family

I used to belong to the church choir at St Michael's and All Angels at Hilperton. The whole family of us were in the choir. We went to Sunday school as children. We used to go twice a day and had outings in the charabancs to Sturton Tower, over near Frome. We didn't go very far because it was the war years. I used to Sunday school teach when I was fourteen or so, there was a group of us. We weren't on our own, the vicar's wife supervised us. She had a lovely singing voice. It was the war years, so they had bring and buy sales, kind of jumble and that. You used to swap things you didn't have any use for. You might do three way swaps to get something you needed. A lot of make do and mend too.

You had a best dress and hat for Sunday and when you got home you had to change it and if you went to church in the afternoon or evening you had to put it back on again. You couldn't run about in it, because money was not as it is today.

Dorothy Walton

Outings

Sunday school outings, yes, we used to go to Clevedon or Burnham or Weston. More often the quieter places. You had a little tag put on you to show you belonged to St Thomas's Sunday school, so you didn't get lost. Sometimes we went on the hills, you know, like for a small outing to Westbury.

Grace Marsden

Sundays at St Thomas's

I often think about it now, we used to have to go early, before church, to morning Sunday school. We had a very nice lady there called Miss Frame. The vicar was a Mr Stimpson. From the Sunday school we had to go into church, for the morning service. The Sunday school was in a building just by St Thomas's. It was a day school during the week, along Brick Platt. Come the afternoon, we had to go to Sunday school again and come evening, we had church again. Every Sunday we had to do that, unless you were ill, you had to go. There was no excuses, so obviously the church was a big thing in your life really. Everybody went to church and every body wore hats. It wasn't right to go into church without a hat, gloves as well and you had Sunday clothes. We weren't allowed to play games on Sundays, we could read, but we weren't allowed to sew. We wouldn't put on a button, nothing like that. We could read books, that was about all.

Grace Marsden

A garden party at St James church in the 1940s is opened by Mrs Forrester. Canon Pelly is seated in the centre.

Trowbridge Sunday school procession passing down Newtown, *c.* 1910.

The Wesley Wailers

At Wesley Road the boys had a good cricket team going on the recreation ground up Silver Street Lane. They were in the local league here before the war. They had a marvellous tennis court up there. Mr James was our Sunday school superintendent, his son was killed in a motorbike accident when he was just eighteen, and in memory of him, he bought this plot of land in Silver Street Lane. He had a pavilion put up and the tennis courts and the cricket pitch done. He had swings put up for the children. That was a very sad occasion, because it was very rare that you heard about a motorbike accident. Tom and the boys were in what they called the Wesley Wailers, putting on concerts. They took them to Westbury and Warminster Methodist churches.

Enid Hill

Fun at the Procession

There used to be huge Sunday school rallies. Every church then had a Sunday school and we all had big banners and from our end of town at Zion, we used to march down and line up in Manvers Street. There were two bands, the front of our part of the procession was the British Legion Boys Band and we would wait there and the other Sunday schools would gather at Trinity Church and they would march up with the Salvation Army band. We would watch their procession go up through the town and we would join on and march up Silver Street and Polebarn Road and go into the park that way. The whole area in front of the bandstand was cordoned off and each Sunday school would have their position. If it was wet, we would march to a local church like Emmanuel. It would be packed out and we'd have to sit in the aisles with seats.

There was one occasion that was quite hilarious. They decided that the two processions instead of joining up, would go different ways. I don't know which way the Trinity one went, but we went down Back Street and we were going to go up Conigre, round British Row and back down Union Street. For some reason something went wrong with Zion. My dad was one of the ones carrying the banner and it had big crowns on the top and when he got round by British Row, it was so narrow, there were trees there, and I think our banner got caught in the trees. By the time we had got it down the rest of the procession was about two hundred yards ahead. It was a boiling hot day and my dad and old Mr Wiltshire, were there in their stiff collars, trying to catch up. We went down Union Street with the rest of the procession way ahead.

Stanley Jones

By Wagon to Tinhead

I went to the Salvation Army until I was about six years old, I had a couple of prizes for going there – for good attendance. Then someone came one day and took me to the Manvers Street Methodist church. They opened a new part for the primary department, that were 1923. I went there until we united with the Tabernacle in 1968. I went right the way through Sunday school, I was Assistant Superintendent when we went over to the Tabernacle church. I was senior steward, yes I went as far as I could go without being a minister. We had Sunday school outings, we used to go to Swanage – usually a charabanc

and then later on, on trains. We went to Severn Beach, when they were trying to make that into a seaside place. We also used to go in Ushers wagons, horse drawn, up to Tinhead and we used to be entertained for tea at Tinhead Methodist church.

Jack Carter

The Lay Preacher

A lay preacher used to come and take the evening service at the church in Whaddon. He was a most unusual man. He used to stand in the pulpit and sway backwards and forwards as he spoke. My mother used to send us

St Stephens church in Castle Street. It was built around 1828 and demolished in 1926.

121

children to this service and occasionally she would take us to Hilperton to a proper service.

Vera Taylor

Silver Jubilee

The Silver jubilee of George and Mary, that was a big occasion. All the Sunday school's were out. We were with Wesley Road and I was holding a banner, there were four of us – two at the front and two at the back, to steady it with this long piece of rope. We paraded right up through Trowbridge into the park. It finished up with a service there. All the school children were given a copy of a book celebrating the King and Queen's Jubilee.

Enid Hill

The Silver Jubilee Sunday school procession on 6 May 1935. The girls holding the Wesley Road banner are Enid Bathard, left, and Irene Lees and the boys are Hector Dyer, left, and Charlie Clark.

The Ship Ha'penny Box

In Sunday school each week we would bring an offering which would go towards expenses like the Sunday school outing and the teaching books we used, but on top of that we would save the halfpennies. There were two lots in circulation – the usual sort with the Queen's head on, but there was also this 'ship ha'penny'. We used to save these 'ship ha'pennies' and send them to missionaries overseas. The ship gave the idea of sending it out overseas, because although there were aeroplanes, most people travelled by sea when they went anywhere of any great distance. We had a large box made of wood with a slot in the top. With my dad being the Superintendent, we used to take great delight when it was so full you couldn't get anymore in. When it was jam packed solid we would count them and bag them and then the box would be empty   and we'd start all over again.

Lynda Bosworth

St James Roof Restored

Inside St James you didn't used to be able to see the roof. It was all dark and black and that. Then they had it restored and painted in 1959 and when it was all done they had a Thanksgiving Service and the Revd Pelly came back to take it. It was his idea you see, but it never got done in his time. The church was packed, absolutely packed. He was a lovely man. For the Coronation they

Denis Taylor, choirboy at St James church in 1928. He later ran the family shop of Taylors in Church Walk.

decorated St James all inside with red, white and blue flowers.

Jessie Whitmarsh

Easter Celebrations

Mrs Hughes got a girls' club going at Newtown school, Friday nights for fourteens onwards from 7 o'clock until 9. She used to have about seventy girls there. We just talked and did little recitations, readings, sing songs and things. She was a great asset to Trowbridge, she went to the Emmanuel Baptist church. She used to get the Easter, Good Friday services off

Manvers Street Methodist church Sunday school in 1950. The picture was taken in the church grounds. The teachers at the back are Joyce Carter (left) and Joan Farr.

the ground. She would arrange for a Christian film in the Gaumont and they would have the Salvation Army Band there and it used to be packed. When the Gaumont was renovated, we went to the Town Hall and then eventually it fizzled out.

Enid Hill

The Conigre Chapel

In the area where we lived there was a church called the Conigre chapel. It was a Baptist church and then it was taken over by the Unitarians. The Conigre church, was a lovely building. When we lived in Upper Broad Street we often went down there on a Sunday

night. A wonderful building – a pity it was pulled down, course it had got delapidated, fewer people were there and eventually the whole area was cleared.

Fred Hardiman

Sunday School Lessons

The afternoon Sunday school would always start with a time of singing choruses, open prayer. If it was any special event coming up you would have a notice section and then you would all go to your individual lessons. Your teacher would usually sit on the end of your row and hopefully keep some kind of order during the first part. When it was class time, instead of being in rows across the room, the forms were then turned around so that you had three to make a little corner against the wall. The girls one side and the boys the other, with a class for the eight year olds, nine, ten and eleven year olds, all round the big Sunday school hall. If there were too many of you then you were privileged to go into the main part of the church and you would sit in the pews and have your lesson.

Generally speaking it was taught in a similar way to lessons at school, from the front. You would sit in your row. You might be required to 'read round' because that was the way we always read the scriptures. You would turn up the pages – you might have your own Bible or you would all have one from the Sunday school, which was sometimes easier if you weren't familiar with the scriptures to be able to find the places.

Lynda Bosworth

Verger at St Thomas's

I heard they were looking for a verger at St Thomas's church and it went with a beautiful little cottage. I went for it and got it. I had to get up early for communion and put the heat on and I had to pull the bell and pump the organ. It was lovely. I had to keep the church clean, naturally and if there was a funeral or a wedding you had to be there to open the doors and give people their hymn books and things like that.

Mavis Burt

Sunday School Anniversaries

Another highlight of the year was the Sunday school anniversary which, at Bethesda, was always the second Sunday in July and that commemorated the starting up of the Sunday school. Other Sunday schools in the town would join you for that day instead of going to their Sunday schools and the church would be packed to capacity. Instead of having the choir in the choir stalls at Bethesda, the oldest in the Sunday school were privileged to sit in the choir stalls. Then they put chairs on the rostrum and extra chairs just to one side if they couldn't all get on the rostrum. All the children would stand and lead the older people in the singing. The hymns would always be chosen by the Sunday school. Sometimes they would have a special set of hymns or songs – little anthems – and sometimes they would be very well known ones or favourite ones that the children enjoyed singing. It was more 'child orientated' and there would be choruses as well. The day before, the Saturday, everybody would bring lots and lots of flowers and they would decorate the whole church. The windowsills would have one large vase and two on either side all the way around the church. Around the pulpit where there was a little ridge, they would put little flower pots, tiny little jam pots with small flowers in. Some people would bring flowers from their gardens or even the common daisy. There were little vases all around the pulpit and the whole church would smell just fantastic. It was one of those celebration days that was done perhaps to excess in some ways.

Lynda Bosworth

The exterior of the old Bethesda chapel in Court Street.

Interior of the old Bethesda chapel in Court Street, later to become part of Salters and presently Dutch Delights in the Shires.